EIGHTEEN WINDOWS TO THE CENTER OF THE UNIVERSE

8/14/2021

To Ernie:
You have the Best
parties –
and a leader

Bill Crossman

bill crossman

Fulton Books, Inc.
Meadville, PA

Published by Fulton Books 2020

ISBN 978-1-64654-784-5 (paperback)
ISBN 978-1-64654-785-2 (digital)

Printed in the United States of America

To Maggie, Ryan, Andrea, and Burke

CONTENTS

Foreword

In this collection of stories, Bill shares his glimpses into the lives of some of the souls that settled in the creatives and idiosyncratic neighborhood of Fremont—sometimes for decades and sometimes for mere moments. Here, Bill gives us the stories of people who rarely get heard and tells of their contributions, some long past and some still to come.

As a near neighbor to Bill and other denizens at the foot of Francis Avenue, I have seen and spoken with some of the people in these pages. Like many readers, I find these folks familiar yet know few of them even though we've lived in proximity. I've been writing about Fremont, as a neighborhood news columnist, for three decades and know a large number of the people here, yet I still find so many slip through the cracks of my understanding.

Through his anecdotes, Bill gives the lives of others a chance to shine forth. He also shows us the universality of their characters and the color of any life. The commodity of character is something Fremont has always had in abundance. Here, Bill shares some of these personalities, but he leaves out a lot of the harsh judgments that too many of us put in the way of meeting and understanding.

The township of Fremont predates the city of Seattle, which swallowed up our predominately blue-collar neighborhood as it grew— then quickly developed a lifetime case of indigestion. Fremont, the neighborhood, has refused to conform on many occasions and then, in the contrary ways of artists and activists, demanded its place at the table. At the start of the third millennium, Fremont has become home to many technology and software businesses, turning our collars more white than blue. Through his eighteen windows, Bill shows that the prosperity of some has made little difference to the true nature of our neighborhood or the people who've found their way to the center of the universe.

Bill describes a Fremont also familiar to me, a lifelong Fremonster, but not mine. He tells about the view from his windows, one that shares his unique outlook. Within his chapters, Bill captures a small slice of his life, served liberally with dollops of the lives of others that he found interesting. Their interest seems to be in their humanity and willingness to talk about it. We all have our stories to tell, but so many will ever be shared. Through his eighteen windows, Bill takes the time to give light and life to a few.

Enjoy the view!

Kirby S. Laney
Fremont Iconologist and Storyteller Publisher
Fremocentrist.com

Acknowledgments

This collection of Fremont stories is the product of several years of Continuing Education writing classes at North Seattle College. I feel fortunate to have instructors Joanne Horne and Steve Lorton and am grateful for their guidance and encouragement.

To my fellow students, particularly Caroline Kennedy, Tamara Pinkas, Jean Swenson, Nora McBride, Gary Lester, Rose Morris, Peter Dudley, Donna Parker, Cynthia Gibbs, and Barbara Reid, a special thanks to Barbara for her work in copy editing the manuscript and to class members' constructive comments.

To employees of the FedEx store in Fremont, a place where thousands of copies were made.

To the characters of Fremont, subjects of stories about them, and their friendship.

To Kirby Lindsey Laney for her cooperation and support and impetus for my start in writing stories about Fremont for Fremocentrist.com.

To readers, thank you for indulging me with these stories, and from my perspective, they've been cheaper than a shrink.

Most of this is true, but as Mark Twain said, "Never let the truth get in the way of a good story."

Fremont Chautauquas: Hindsight

In the state of Washington, city of Seattle, there is Fremont. Since the 1970s, it is self-proclaimed as the center of the universe, also known to its denizens as the Artist's Republic of Fremont, or ARF. And today, it is known as a place that attracts and appeals to quirky, creative neighbors with the ethos to embrace and tolerate revival. The motto "De Libertas Quirkas" is painted on the rocket. "The freedom to be peculiar" gives permission and license. The urban village is likely best known for the annual Solstice Parade with the lead of hundreds of naked bicyclists.

Chautauqua is an Iroquois word that has a few meanings, but in my Fremont, they are gatherings and/or events where a common lesson is learned as a takeaway.

But like it or likely not, in the past ten years, Seattle has boomed loudly in and around us in Fremont. This era will be the pig in the python of a growing metropolis' evolution.

My stories, my memories, my experiences follow our lives here at the foot of Francis Avenue in the twenty-first-century center of the universe.

I look out a front door with eighteen windows on the rest of the world; conversely, the eighteen windows allow the world to look in on me.

For me, Fremont unfolds and reveals itself with each walkabout, like in John Steinbeck's mid-twentieth-century classic *Cannery Row* when describing Monterey, California. I'll draw comparisons to his work here: Fremont, like Monterey, is a *poem* of fun, not *fish, a stink* like roasting beans from Theo's Chocolates, *a grating noise* with sirens and honky-tonks disguised as brewpubs, music venues, and sirens, did I say? With the thump of the bass guitars from bands of musicians on the way up and the way down the charts and combined with the cacophony of festivals and endless nightlife no matter what time of day.

It's a *tone* as in a harmonic pulse, *a habit* as in twenty-five years of Fremont Sunday Market, a funky collector's dream. *A nostalgia* like the row of houses turned storefronts along Thirty-Sixth Avenue that made necessary a new story meeting the current street level when they raised Thirty-Sixth Avenue in 1911 to build the Fremont Bridge. *A dream* or a nightmare to those jumpers including my neighbor Bitsy who survived from meeting her demise in the waters below the Aurora Bridge on Highway 99, which officially is the George Washington Memorial Bridge.

Fremont, like Monterey, has evolved from *lumber and canned sardines* to computer applications and software. Instead of *whores, pimps, and gamblers*, it got hippies, geeks, millennials, and hood rats bumping into us without apology by not taking the time to look away from their cell phones or show moderate concern when their little precious pooch shits on the parking strips or their beverage of choice container is discarded on the curb as they fight for the planet. It's *sons of bitches* to the Sons of Norway and everyone in between.

Like the flawed colorful denizens of *Cannery Row*, Fremont has the equivalent intensity of resident expressionists.

I'm awakened this fine day by the sound of Bitsy's voice. I share a wall with her and Marshall in my funky fourplex at the foot of Francis Avenue. She's one of five surviving bridge jumpers. With her raspy cigarette voice, she talks baby talk to her love of fourteen years, Marshall. I see her out front as I water the fuchsias and clean up the mess from that rascal raccoon, who digs up my flower beds and threatens the plants that the snails and slugs haven't eaten yet. I empty beer into small shallow vessels to tempt their suicidal fates.

Legend has it when hitting the water after jumping from the bridge (since lined with a tall fence), the houseboat people came out and said, "Are you all right?"

"No!" she yells while bobbing in the deep. "I'm so goddamned fucking mad I'm still alive."

I learned a lesson from Bitsy when she caught me in my garden later that morning, wiping tears from my eyes. A close relative of mine was hospitalized from a suicide attempt. Bitsy proceeded with a confiding tone to tell me of her four attempts and her voice of experience, twice slitting her wrists.

She said, "Go see them in the hospital. Tell them how much they are loved and how you want to have them remain on this earth. *But* in two weeks, you see her again, bring other family members, and you *kick* her ass all the way to Ballard, and tell her how she fucked up your lives with this decision."

"Bill," Bitsy cautioned, "remember, it's not a question of if she'll try again. It's a question of when." I'm shaken, tear up again, plead with fate, but get the message that I look out for me too.

"It's good advice," I tell Bitsy, who walks at a slant, which is almost as wide as she is tall.

She tells me "We like *our* beer."

I say, "I like beer too."

"*No. We really* like our beer," she emphasizes.

"How so?" I say.

"We drink a case or two each day."

Bitsy's heart is her guide to life, more so than her mind and her body.

Also, I'm joined on the sidewalk by Benny, walking purposely to his slice of the universe at the storefront with the "Photo Engravers" signage. Benny asks me if I have a buck or two to loan him. *Loan?* I think. He'll buy Old English Ale, drinking the high-octane beer to start the day. The storefront is a loose neighborhood secret. It's a performance and recording studio for artists like Pearl Jam and Dave Matthews. Dizzy, the busker, asked me to help him with his recording sessions there.

Like he has almost every day for over twenty years, Benny, the self-proclaimed "Monk of Fremont," stacks and balances rocks using the parking strip and sidewalk as most days he sits as a sentinel. "Benny" Benhariz whose last name is Libyan for "Son of a Tinkerer." The "Rock dancer" is another term he uses as a description of his performance art.

Benny Benhariz, Rock Dancer, the Monk,
and Unofficial Mayor of Fremont.

Later this afternoon, likely Benny will shift from quiet drunk to full-on rant and rave all night long in the mostly politically tinged, crack-fueled, right-out-of-the-headlines, worldview musings. See the story on the "Unofficial Mayor."

I hear a rattle on the other side of the chain-link fence next door. I don't look up, with full realization that those residing in the adjacent apartment building are an odd lot, many antisocial, armed with their defenses, except for one, the "Mother Superior," I call her, not knowing her Christian name. For fear of pissing her off, I say nothing. She's dressed in her usual long smock jumper, orthopedic shoes, and chopped hair. She frequently has a strident quick pace in her steps. And when she speaks, she rarely makes eye contact. On this occasion, she purrs in my direction, in a rare appearance, addressing me and my garden of organisms, gewgaws, crows, raccoon, sparrows, petunias, and marigolds struggling for the right to grow and thrive. "Like Matisse," she says, still staring at the recycle bin, "you rely on bright colors."

"Aww, shucks," I say, in return with my left hand outstretched to point out my "memorial to my demons." "This garden is cheaper than a shrink," I say to her. "Thank you so very much."

The Mother Superior monitors the proximity as the unofficial busybody of plants and the garbage disposal for this part of the block and seems to know who's good and who's not. My last interchange with her, she was going on about my contributions to the garden here, making impressive compliments I didn't deserve. Mother Superior gushed over some salvaged stack of glass from some Dale Chihuly-inspired Groupon glass blowing class held nearby.

"Oh, that," I say. I discount the glass, and I guess her compliment as well. Later that next day, I mysteriously find it pulled apart, and the glass ball is broken and thrown in a pile of discarded weeds. I suspect I crossed an imaginary line of her neighborly social conventions.

Matisse? I think to myself. My head swells another hat size.

I head out onto Thirty-Sixth Avenue north to do my routine walkabout through the center of the universe to my bank. There's the work of Juan Casanova.

The Guerilla Gardener

Plucked out of a Cuban prison, serving time for murder, in Fidel Castro's 1980 discharging of his incarcerated and insane citizens on boats bound for Miami. Juan found his way to Seattle, via a prison term in Wisconsin, as a cook. In a refreshing (to most) effort, the guerrilla gardener is a lone operative. He plants and maintains, as a gift to the community, the sidewalks and parking strips with flowers, fountains, and bright groupings of vegetation to beautify our universe.

Well-kept begets well-kept in the sidewalk wars, I've found. In the Fremont night scene, this pushes the yard line to the business' benefit. The littering of beer containers, bottles, and sundry junk by our "guests," many of which are our best and brightest college students, is disquieting. It's an irony that some socially stunted idiots, ready to save the earth, after just a couple polite snorts of Jägermeister—far from the view of their university, parents at home and prospective employers—continue to trash, throw, cast away, damage, or tag with spray paint graffiti.

After a fire destroyed his old building at the Leary curve, Juan was asked if he wanted to rent a room above the Fremart, which was formerly called M&S Deli, in Lloydeen's old apartment. Except now, it was one room, not the two, with one single bathroom for all tenants to share in the old Fremont Hotel.

Juan Casanova's calling to guerilla gardening fulfills his need to do something for the community, to leave a legacy, with a check on materialism with "just necessities," he mused, and kindness toward others. "Life is full in Fremont."

Juan Casanova: The
Guerilla Gardener

In Casanova's sharing of his heart, in his distinct Cuban dialect, he asserts passionately, "I live La Pura Vida," and "love each day by day." He bristles at other's pursuits to own more "things." I ask him if he knows his neighbors. He extends his arm and makes a sweeping motion. "I know everybody... *everybody*. Where are the families? We need more families. There are no children." Since 2013, Juan has connected the west end of Thirty-Sixth Avenue businesses to the foot of Francis with his guerrilla plantings in the eight-foot parking strips that line it. Gardens have been erected one day and removed the next.

Juan confers his work with or without property owners and with or without their permission. He labors with intent given as a purely altruistic gesture. His gestures cause reaction gestures in others. He gets testy when asked where his plants come from. I ask him, "What would you like to be remembered for when you are gone?"

Without missing a beat, he clearly expresses with direct eye contact and pointed index finger, "That I was a *mean* motherfucker!"

Lately, for the last six months or so, Juan hasn't been seen much. He seems to stay up in his room with the walls and ceiling and the hotel stairway covered in his religious icons and poetry of life. In January of 2019, Juan was awarded "Fremont Citizen of the Year" by a vote of the residents and business readers of Fremocentrist.com.

Drink a toast to human kindness, recognition, and trophies. Juan Casanova.

Flying Touch and Go with Francis' Foot

It all closed in on Lloydeen, sixty-ish, a friend, a tenant of Moses (when he operated the M&S Deli Mart and rented rooms above). With current owner-operators, her practice of paying rent in dribs and drabs was intolerable. She was handed an invitation to uninhabit by new owners, brothers Ron and John. Her move away from the foot of Francis Avenue was sealed when her car was "booted" and held ransom by the city of Seattle for overdue fees and warrants. She walked away from both.

Without home or car, her boyfriend, in a cougar case study, was prompted to move in with his dad, who had an even bigger alcohol problem.

Lloydeen's sneak of a canine, Frida, an Australian border collie who would steal your sandwich when you took your eyes off it. If there was no food served, there was always compost in the garden if the dog was out and the kitchen countertops if roamed free in.

Lloydeen was and is an entrepreneur, making her living off the grid from "the Bins" (the nickname for the Goodwill Outlet Store in SODO). Lloydeen, out of dedication or need for survival, arrived there weekdays by 7:30 a.m., picked a number, and lined up for the most giant brawl and combat shopping exercises seen in these parts. Security supervised, with the time pressure of a game show, a guild of dedicated scavengerneers search for items sold by the pound. All added up and told, her inventory of saleable would be offered on eBay, ETSY, at the Fremont Vintage Mall, and the Fremont Sunday Market.

Once, she found a painting that later sold at Sotheby's Auction for $14,000, and another time a silver tray that resold for $1,200. With Lloydeen's trained eye and iPhone (when the bill has been paid), she finds items to reprice and repurpose. A former methamphetamine user, now on prescription Adderall, she finds solace at one of the few remaining dive bars to down whiskeys most nights. Things just haven't been the same since the Buckaroo and The Dubliner taverns left the neighborhood.

Carrying the baggage and reputation of a sloppy drunk, Lloydeen has the innate ability to suck all the oxygen out of a room with a mouth ten times as powerful as her eyes and ears. With a cigarette fueled deep raspy voice, she was easily mimicked by the actor in a play written by her gay ex-husband about their Italian honeymoon, performed at the west of Lenin Theater here in Fremont.

Diminutive in stature and weight, she keeps her hair meticulously coifed at shoulder length but has a nervous habit of flicking it back like a teenager with Tourette's. Lloydeen and I became acquainted when she was driving a school bus, and we were both vendors at Fremont Sunday Market. Like her dog, Frida, she's developed the skill to mooch with slow but incremental intensity from the moochee to the moocher.

She has a penchant for gossip. More than once, I was caught in some conflict with others in the neighborhood because of what she said.

When she had to attend her son's wedding in North Carolina a few years ago, much like the Bette Davis character in the movie *A Pocket Full of Miracles*, I was Glenn Ford as we tried to doll her up to the image she needed to pull off that gig. We couldn't get her missing front teeth fixed, but she adapted with a pursed lips demeanor that impressed the bride's family.

Lloydeen's reminded me a few times how we should be married. *Not* a chance. She'll always be a friend, but like her approach to paying her rent, she's better in dribs and drabs.

She's since rented a small garage apartment near the shore in Magnolia. Her landlord is an older woman that married quite well—so well that she's a Republican. I wish Lloydeen blue skies, but already, there are signs of stress and storms. In her daily struggles, I choose anonymity.

Mobile now with another car, life is picking up. She was in the neighborhood recently and stopped by like an old friend. I filled her with whiskey and made her dinner. Uncharacteristically, she did the dishes after. Later, I would see the damage done to that bottle of forty-year-old whiskey I kept on the shelf.

Lloydeen seems much calmer now and seems to take solace in the natural sea air of Puget Sound. New life as grandmother and recipient of social security are two roles she has embraced. I miss not having her close by.

The Unofficial Mayor: The Monk of Fremont

My first impressions of Benny are scorched into memory. Moving here to Fremont from Newcastle, I first lived up the block in the town house I shared with the colonel. Ten years ago seems a long time, but it's a blink of an eye. When the colonel wasn't yelling, drilling, or spilling, I would encounter this towering figure with the dreadlocks shouting and politicizing his rants in front of the recording studio on Thirty-Sixth Avenue.

The studio has signage that says, "Photo Engravers." Inside is an open two-story recording and performing venue for artists like Pearl Jam and Dave Matthews. It has a beautiful chandelier and is circled in full-height drapes. Dizzy's had recording sessions there, and I had cause to ogle the plush studio with Benny standing palace guard most days and most nights for the past twenty-three years. Dizzy needed some help to transport the equipment within spitting distance to the studio. My car was the camel, and on this day, I channel and become the Gladys Kravitz* of the neighborhood. Dizzy has his own story too.

Benny's voice is gravelly and hoarse most nights and like butter and honey most days. It was unsettling to the nerves. During the days, when I encountered this tall, dreadlocked, larger-than-life figure, I would cross the street intentionally so as not to cross his path or risk him taking me on. I didn't want to give him a reason nor a hint that I had the desire to flee.

One day, he was walking by my place while I was cutting the grass. I couldn't run indoors, so I ignored this figure of my avoidance. Instead, Benny walked over to me, looked me in the eye, and told me, "Your garden is beautiful."

I gave a brief curious response, "Thank you. We've put a lot of work into it."

From then on, our relationship was that of fellow Fremonsters. Benny revealed his Libyan heritage immigrating to the United States after studying at Loyola University. He speaks five languages. He knows and respects "Ms. Jude," my aunt, and her daughter and granddaughter. Aunt Jude has her stories as well.

This familial connection added to my stock value in the network of denizens at the foot of Francis Avenue. It also made me a ready soft target for donating dollars to their causes like alcohol during the daylight and something stronger in the night. The inebriated nighttime is when Benny propels his rants to epic proportions. I justified my donations as insurance so that he would have my back and give warnings if some of the other street urchins had designs on my person and belongings. This established Fremonster seemed to be accepting of the colonel and me as domestic partners and new Fremonsters. The colonel is referenced here and there, but the story hasn't been told.

Truth be told, Benny has been at the same location from early morning till after the bars closed for twenty-three years. Yes, twenty-three. The casual observer, and most who've spent any time in Fremont, know of Benny but as a homeless street man, a performance artist, and a stacker of rocks or his self-designated "Rock Dancer." Benny's fascination and talent with rock sculptures began because of a traumatic experience at age five when his older brother was killed at Benghazi University in a bloody protest demonstration. His play with rocks soothed young Benny. He finds truth in a quote he attributes to Charles Bukowski, "Art will save yourself from madness."

Benny describes three parts of his art: (1) artistic expression— express oneself artistically every day; (2) Newtonian physics of gravity; and (3) the spiritual and cultural connection to the object. He is quick to say, "Rocks live in the eternal nowness" and "Rocks are an early human commodity and from the big bang that created everything including humans."

"I keep an eye on the rocks in my garden," I tell him, "and before I bring a rock home or play a casino slot machine, it must speak to me."

I say to Benny, "After twenty-three years here on the street, you're famous!"

He prefers to say, "I'm quite famous, but not rich. I'm reviving an art form that belongs to humanity."

I usually introduce Benny to family and friends with a mention that he is the unofficial mayor of Fremont. And he'll say, "And Bill is the lover of Fremont." I blush and am speechless at that remark. Benny, on the other hand, tells me has been celibate for the last seventeen years. The females who live at this end of the street might challenge that notion.

We remember Salvador, a.k.a. Bongo Man, whose station was across the street from Benny's. Salvador, from El Salvador, a veteran of the United States Army, was a friend of Benny's as they shared the foot of Francis Avenue for thirteen years. By day, Salvador was positioned with his Old English Ale (OE) and a tattered Bible to read and quote, occasionally passing out on the sidewalk on sunny afternoons. And out front of the Nectar Lounge music venue by night till the wee hours of the morning singing, slapping his drums, elusive to the beat of the music. We both missed him and shared a fond remembrance moment. Last year, one night, Salvador went to the hospital and died suddenly. No known survivors.

The drummer tangled with the old fart who didn't smile and lived briefly above the Fremart with a packed gun. The old fart didn't stay but a few weeks here. You'd think while coming and going and while walking his little lap dog, he could acknowledge those of us with neighborly proximity. Salvador would sometimes sleep on the back stairs of the Fremart or use the back-lawn wall as a toilet. The old fart with the SUV dumped a gallon of maple syrup under the big tree in front of Nectar Lounge that was Salvador's nighttime station. Most nights, Salvador was feeling no pain or in a stupor playing his drum with out-of-rhythm beats to the band on the legendary neighborhood stage. The syrup attracted ants from all over the city to descend upon the tree's base. The old fart moved away shortly after Salvador's death.

Benny and I hypothesize Salvador's demise and speculate the old fart being a hired gun. I bet it was imitation maple syrup. Benny led a memorial service for his friend under that sticky tree. We left flowers and notes written to honor his place as another palace guard. We reaffirm our belief that even homeless lives matter.

There was a time before that Benny, Salvador, and I were at odds with each other. When I assumed the crown to the Speed Queen Laundromat until its doors were shuttered three years ago, both men would use the unattended business as a place to hang out on those rainy days. I was compelled to expel them from this practice as the alcohol and their spirits hurt business, particularly among female customers. I pushed, and they pushed back at me for doing a job. Salvador would take chairs from the business to set outside if he couldn't hang in the laundry. He was joined by a few others, sometimes Benny too in verbal lashings, taunting me, much like one would receive in junior high school from the moron class bully. I bit my tongue but stopped my donations to their causes during this Laundromat phase of my life. The Speed Queen Coin Laundry has her story as well.

Benny and I talk about more of our fellow characters and try to make sense of it. I mention Bitsy and her jump from the Aurora Bridge. We marvel at her surviving the jump that ended in the water hundreds of feet below. Bitsy, a short, stout woman, Benny says she had a new nickname after that—"Duck Squasher."

Benny asked me if I knew Merle.

"I don't recall," I say, "he must have been before my time."

"He was a big man," Benny laments, "clumsy, sensitive but with a good heart. People didn't take him seriously." Merle lived down on the banks of the ship canal. Benny, the rock dancer, didn't go with him that day when Merle asked for help to move his stuff to another place on the canal. The community was shocked and surprised to see and hear him jump from the bridge to his death on the concrete below.

Two years ago, the state finally put up a deterrent fence on that bridge that had been built in 1932.

Juan, the guerrilla gardener, Benny, and Dizzy, the rocker, all have discussed erecting a memorial to the 230 suicide jumpers who, unlike Bitsy, met their demise from the bridge's charms. Here told, the first thought of a jumper after their feet leave the guardrail is that of regret.

Benny is always with a couple of books under the arm. He projects a pastoral presence with loose-fitting shoes or sandals, pants and light jacket, and with a beret on top of dreadlocked dark hair.

He believes he lives a pastoral lifestyle, but some of us don't see it.

A serious naturalized US citizen and voter, Benny was pressed into service during the Iraq War as an Arabic interpreter for the military. More than once, frequently actually, this preacher, Benny, the Monk of Fremont, has made a comment related to life in the center of the universe that is so profound to me that his words are steeped in emotion and power and land in the upfront part of my head. His regret is a useful state of mind, vacating the feelings and body made hollower. We make every attempt to mitigate it if we're human. And we avoid the doorways that cause it, and we are alternately attracted.

Conscience is a bad thing to waste, ya think? We overthink if we're among the smartest of us and smart if we overthink this.

This past winter, this enterprising man of the street took his craft of the rock sculptures to the shores of Oahu. He proved he could maintain static existence through his art, and possible franchise ideas came next.

Benny's absence from the foot of Francis was immediately felt with lots of speculation to his whereabouts during his trip to Paradise. The Monk, Benny, returned in March near the equinox. While it was a cold spring to his squat of many seasons on the parking strip of Thirty-Sixth Ave, despite the cold and graffiti taggers' damage to his mural painted on the storefront, he seemed excited for his homecoming.

A friend of his was delivering rocks and small boulders the day when we first met this spring. He was perched on his rocks awaiting the delivery. Benny is a curmudgeon by night and monk by day. He is known by many residents and visitors to these parts.

Benny changes and challenges our beliefs and values on behalf of what we designate and count as the homeless in this city.

Benny's friend pulls up in a white van, I welcome him back. We caught each other up on known news, and I tell him we need to erect a statue of him.

"Benny, the troll monk of Fremont."

We both laugh full of guffaws. I let out a cackle that even surprises me, sounding a boyish glee. We reach out our arms and hug each other goodbye.

I repeat again to him to include my earnest notion of erecting a statue to Benny as a parting shot and attempt at quantum humanity.

This time, it only cost me five bucks. Tomorrow, I'll try to get him to take my $1.29 church organ away. It'll assist in his pastoral work.

Moses and M&S Deli

Moses Shaibi

Here at the foot of Francis, for thirty-three years, Moses Shaibi was the operator of the M&S Deli. From 1983 until 2016. Every day, every day, right here in the Fremont Hotel Building.

He recalls the Baby Diaper Service, located next door, the Tyler Dog Food Company located here in the neighborhood.

Moses recalls so much history. Red Hook Brewery started in a small room down the block before moving to the Trolley Barn. The Seattle City Sanitation Department used the building and grounds during Fremont's light industrial era. That old trolley barn is now home to the Theo Chocolate factory, source of the sweet smell of roasting chocolate in the neighborhood. One catches a waft on good days walking about.

Oh yes, he remembers the hippies. "The Deli," as neighbors called it, offered a dynamic product assortment for neighborhood Fremonsters and fuel for nighttime reveler's thirsts.

Front door and interior shelves of M&S Deli built as the Fremont Hotel at the foot of Francis.

The storefront door, simultaneously facing Thirty-Sixth Avenue and Francis Avenue north, is surrounded by an early twentieth-century building that has full cold storage, basement, industrial kitchen, rooms to rent, shared bath and water closet. There's also a service window for the late-night demographic.

Stairways, both north and south, connect the second-floor corridor. The front doors open to a wide stairway, revealing a well-lit atrium with a massive skylight. Interior walls, ceiling, woodwork, some flooring, and fixtures are original 1920s craftsman-style construction.

Lloydeen's sneaky canine
on interior stairway of the
old Fremont Hotel.

As if frozen in time, the building also shows the wear of time. Outside walls reveal layers of paint overs of graffiti taggers' handiworks that are markers of territory like dogs doing the same. There's an occasional sighting of shoes tied together by the shoestrings looped over the power lines as symbols of gang recruit's rites of initiation.

Behind the building, there's a grassy square for residents' vehicles bordered by the brick wall of Nectar Lounge and the larger-than-life mural titled *A Monument to Digital Divinity*. The mural, painted by artist Jeff Jacobson, also now has the permanent augmentation of the tagger's handiwork.

What if these interior and exterior walls could talk? There's the feeling here they do!

These remnants, refuse, and revelers of each day's and night's street scene make one day blend into the next. This building, with a stubborn adaptation to life a hundred years later, could be a preservationist's dream. The southeast corner of the building over the doorway seems to be buckling under the weight carried all those years.

Moses was born in Yemen with the biblical name. And like Lee Chong, the Chinese grocer portrayed in John Steinbeck's 1945 book *Cannery Row,* Moses was a central character in a *colorful gallery of unforgettable denizens.* Like Chong, in another era, Moses offered more personal credit accounts, yet both similarly understood building community was one of the bottom lines. To paraphrase Steinbeck, not that Moses was avaricious, he wasn't, but if one wanted to spend money, he was available.

Moses earned his US citizenship in the milestone US Bicentennial year of 1976. He proudly remarked this to anyone who might question his Middle Eastern origin.

Lloydeen, one of his tenants and a Fremont Sunday Market vendor, described Moses as a generous, concise, big-hearted gentleman who was also the landlord-merchant of Fremont at the foot of Francis. He was often heard speaking perfect English or his native Arabic on his cell phone. He and his wife, Nicole, his childhood sweetheart, have raised four successful bilingual, dual citizenship adult children here.

Photo of two former tenants Dizzy and Lloydeen.

Like most naturalized US citizens, Moses took the responsibility of voting participation very seriously. The television above the door always had the cable news stations on. He loved to talk politics with anyone, especially his neighbors, who might have time to linger at the counter.

For many of us whose citizenship is merely a birthright and a registration, we tend to take it all for granted. But consider for Moses and his network of extended family, their citizenship is earned. It is acquired by a circuitous journey from their first arrival on the shores to navigating the Immigration and Naturalization Service, taking classes in English and US government, and passing a culminating exam. Their sponsors and their ethnic group more than often make a commitment to pay back and pay it forward to others.

My aunt Jude and her daughter and cousin Anna helped Moses in the deli. They were the face of the deli counter during the lunch hour. Moses called Aunt Jude "Goo-dee." Jude is no stranger to politics and political involvement. I surmise there were many ongoing political conversations among them.

This counter, where a political discussion was overheard, was the site of one of my life-changing center of the universe magic moments to be described later.

Through Moses's thirty-three years of our day to day, the night-life, festivals, and events that are the stuff of legends, Moses and his extended family served neighbor denizens, destination revelers, and passersby and passers-through. They were there from our first-morning hit of caffeine to our last of the night's shot with most things incidental between—every day, every morning, and every night.

Like Steinbeck's Chong, Moses's M&S Deli *was the place to go for your stuff.*

When asked about his dreams for his future as he approached retirement age, he says, "*Futures.* I'll be here, what else would I do?"

In 2015, fending off multiple offers to sell in Seattle's real estate boom, he quietly, overnight, sold the business to Ron and John, who also run the 7-Eleven convenience store one block west. Their children and extended family now operate the market as the Fremart. The service window is now a convenience food lovers' dream operated as Fremont Food by their extended family residing here near the foot of Francis Avenue.

Portions of this story were published in the *Fremocentrist*, our neighborhood online news source. It was subsequently translated into five languages. Just a small testament to a man and his dedication to serving his neighbors and Fremont's guests.

Quietly, Moses changed his name to Abu and lives now in an unidentified Midwest major city known for cheap real estate and out-of-work union autoworkers. We miss him, but those are the rules of the witness protection program. (Just joking.)

At the time, when this goes into publication, the fate of the Fremart is unknown. It'll be end of business as we know it in early spring 2020. The old Fremont Hotel building is in disrepair and needs major structural work to survive in a city drunk on the boom of new residents and a penchant for tearing it down, digging a hole, and erecting a structure for the nameless and faceless future—a future characterized by online orders and deliveries to our door and mouths.

A First of Many Center of the Universe Moments: Aunt Jude

Sometimes, stars and planets align here in the center of the universe, and synchronicity occurs. "Welcome to Fremont—Watch Out for Déjà Vu," as the street sign reads.

Waiting behind the diminutive woman in line who was having a political discussion with Moses, at the counter in the deli, was made more urgent because I'd left my dog, Argo, with a young girl who offered outside the front door.

The store was the corner store, a block away from my first Fremont home on Dayton Avenue.

A beautiful spring day it was in April 2007. To try to move the line along, I smile and say to the woman, "Gee, it's a lovely day out there." The woman seems to bristle and appears to either ignore me or rebuff me for trying to hit on her. Moses patiently stands behind the counter.

An instant later, I caught a glimpse of her eye to eye. Her sparkling blue eyes were prominent through a weathered face that revealed a hint of premature aging like any other baby boomer surviving their excesses. Her shoulder-length hair was a blond and silver mix.

Lightning struck me right there. I said to her in an astonished tone, "Judy? Judy Crossman?"

I wasn't sure if my memory serves me well at this point because I remembered her with bright red hair.

Now it is her turn to be hit by a lightning bolt. I've startled her. She remains silent.

"It's Bill Crossman, your nephew."

A memory flood rolls over me. From my earliest memory, Judy Lee was like a sister, just three years older.

"Jude," she corrects me, "Jude Crossman Morford."

"That's right," I say nervously.

We exchange how-are-yous and give each other the obligatory look overs and a cautious hug.

"I'm just out walking the dog," I say. "I moved up the block a few months ago on Dayton."

She counters, "Why, I live on the block as well."

Truth be told, it's been fifty-two years since we last saw each other in our birthplace, Tacoma.

The little girl who offered to watch my dog is Gabrielle, seven, my second cousin. Her mother, Anna, is a cousin I've not met. As kids in the 1950s and early 1960s, Jude was my hero. She led me to church and popular culture. Listening to 45 RPM records, we danced "The Twist." She taught me to dance the "Mashed Potato" like other kids caught up in the Gidget, Patty Duke, American Bandstand era. At ten, I took my first jet plane ride with her to visit Aunt Barbara and Aunt Marilyn, her sisters, in Los Angeles.

Now it is Moses's turn to share in the lightning strikes and collective astonishment.

Was this a chance reunion of coincidence? Or was it the universe unfolding as it should? Irony, this meeting occurred in Fremont, the center of the universe.

We step outside the store, gather up the dog, and I'm introduced to Gabrielle. With a lot of kid questions made and explanations that couldn't be made, we cross Francis Avenue to her home in the funky fourplex.

We exchange phone numbers with good intentions demonstrated. We both appear to lower our expectations for a possible familial relationship.

"Please call me," she says as we part.

"Don't worry, I'm not going to lose you a second time after all these years!"

The heartfelt response made while still reeling in a state of surprise.

A little or too much of the backstory now. Jude was my dad's youngest sibling. My parents, Bill Sr. and Gladys, split up in 1964 shortly after my mom gave birth to my youngest brother, Joe. They owned the Horseshoe Tavern near the city hall in Tacoma. It was a messy uncoupling. We were played by both sides as pawns, receptacles of adult anger, angst, pride, and vitriol for each other. Gladys married the beer truck driver, John, a wonderful man. After selling the tavern, my dad faked his disappearance to Alaska with the help of my uncle Bud. Bill Sr.'s entire family, aunts, uncles, cousins, and even grandma broke with my brothers and me, and it would leave a void in mine and myself. I always assumed my dad used this deception to keep from paying child support.

Later, he was found, by accident, when the sheriff called my mom. Bill was living in North Cove on the ocean with his Minit Mart, Minit Manor triplexes, and the Costa Plenty Ranch with his second wife, Lydia. They had two miniature horses that got a lot more attention than her two sons. Their neglect fueled time for her two boys to do crimes and incarcerations. Lydia was chained to the store while Bill served four terms as county commissioner.

Now back to 2007. In a giddy turn of the universe, Aunt Jude was back in my life.

Too much time had passed simply to pick up our relationship where we left off in our teenage years. We knew it was time to put any twentieth-century family dramas to rest, most of which were out of our control.

To the denizens at the foot of Francis Avenue, she's still known as Ms. Jude and the woman who ran the Speed Queen Laundromat and worked the counter at M&S Store and Deli. To Moses, she's known as "Goo-dee."

And to thousands of listeners of national talk show radio programs, she's known as Jude, a frequent caller, a titan of late-night progressive political talk radio.

Jude's ability to touch lives still resonates here at the foot of Francis. She moved away from Fremont and the funky fourplex about ten years ago after inheriting a nice chunk of money from her brothers' estates. This was also the point in my life to leave my first Fremont address and the relationship that was intertwined.

I saw the opportunity and felt the need to remain here and assumed my stewardship of the same address in the funky fourplex. This month, it'll be ten years.

Recently, we met in her new home outside Tacoma to discuss this process of writing. Initially, it was my goal to determine if there were any common threads, despite huge gaps in our familial relationships, that might give evidence to our shared DNA.

The Irish/English origins of our last name: it is the man who is close to the cross or the man who gets you across.

Jude's dad, my grandfather and namesake, was an engineer for the Milwaukee Road Railroad. He subsequently died of a heart attack behind the controls of the engine with a mile of the train behind it down Snoqualmie Pass. The freight train started acting erratically, and the conductor came forward and found him dead.

My uncle Bob, Jude's brother, became an Amtrak conductor on the Coast Starlight, retired, and moved to Hawaii and was murdered in a love triangle.

I have a passion for career and technical education and training students for workplace success.

Jude's career was the ultimate leading of others across the dimensions as a hospice nurse, or midwife to the dying. She fills her time in retirement with her grandkids and working the counter of a family-owned candy store.

Jude, a force of nature with childlike tendencies, she is a one-woman tour de force for justice. She admits she has too much empathy. She's a political movement activist with her founding of Womenstanding, an organization for peace.

Readers will see her spirit and presence threaded throughout these stories of those who live at the foot of Francis Avenue, Fremont, center of the universe, city of Seattle.

Cousin Julie, Jude, and J. P. Patches statue late for the Interurban.

Bill in his $5 tux with Aunt Jude.

EZ Friendship

When I asked when his birthday was at age thirty-four, he turned out to be a Cancer on the astrology signs. That meant he's the person we all tell our secrets to. They're approachable. My brother, Mark, is a Cancer too, and he tells tales of complete strangers approaching on the street to share their darkest secrets to him. It struck me as we got to know each other better that EZ's birthday, July 2, was the same as my maternal Croatian grandpa. Coincidence, but it was as if EZ was channeling Grandpa with his frequent use of the colloquialism, "whatchamacallit."

You could see his eyeballs look up and back in his head as he used his favorite term instead of finding the right word to describe his world that spread from the International District to Belltown, to Palm Springs to Fremont, to West Seattle, to Tukwila, and back again to Fremont.

EZ was born in Oakland, California, situated in the birth order between two sisters with a beautiful white mother and a black father. He spent his childhood in Portland, earning his street smarts and doing time in group homes when everything went south after his father was murdered. He describes his dad as a doppelgänger for the boxer with the bedroom eyes, Evander Holyfield. He's grateful to someone at an early age, who diverted his trajectory in crime and gang banging to his life today.

EZ inherited those eyes and a build many might describe as a "brick shit house." He's solid, defined, and today is forty-three years of age and one of my best friends, a confidant. EZ is like family in my solar system here in the center of the universe.

As my abusive relationship was crumbling, EZ and I met, had a date, and it was a nonstop session of words, ideas, and for me, much older, flattering to have the attention of a much-younger man. He casually mentioned being in a porn film. I let that one drift over my head.

Later, while still living in my Fremont town house, I happened into a Capitol Hill gay bar and was astonished to see an X-rated gay porn film he was starring in, projected on the wall. I said, "*Look!* It's that hunk, EZ." This was no sleazy amateur porn flick; it was a big-budget production by one of the big studios, and EZ was billed as a studio-exclusive. The industry nominated him in that production year for best new artist. He instead was honored with "best scene." He was an innovator of style and looks. His tattoos and demeanor and talents were recognized around the world when he toured Japan and Europe. He was surprised when fans recognized him on the streets. His turn of the century work spanned a half dozen films. He was cast as a drifter, thug, carney, and finally, a prison escapee, shackled and handcuffed. It was a persona he knew was a direction he didn't want to take his career. And despite fans wanting more, he retired in an industry with no reputation for residual incomes.

For me, at age fifty-eight, I was in the throes of what turned out to be a messy gay divorce. My ex, "The Colonel" with his master's degree in war knew that continuing to keep me in court would put me on the defensive, and he would gain ground and my share of the town house we shared.

Friends expressed their sympathy for me as I struggled.

But it was those words I savored and proudly spouted in response, likely in a sheepish bragging voice, "I am dating an international gay porn star." EZ preferred simply white men age fifty and over. My emotions ran the gamut from exhilaration, walking on air to "there's no fool like an old fool." If you can pull it off, I'd recommend the ride. EZ has a "je ne sais quoi" (that particular something I cannot describe) about himself, a certain charisma one can't explain. I have never had a friend or colleague or family member that has my back. EZ commanded my respect that grew stretched when there were little self-development efforts made or completed. And EZ's show business name was Dred Scott.

(The Dred Scott decision was the Supreme Court's ruling on March 6, 1857, that having lived in a free state and territory did not entitle a slave, Dred Scott, to his freedom. In essence, the decision argued that as a slave, Scott was not a citizen and could not sue in a federal court. The majority opinion by Chief Justice Roger B. Taney also stated that Congress had no power to exclude slavery from the territories [thus invalidating the Missouri Compromise of 1820] and that African Americans could never become US citizens.)

By choosing Dred Scott, EZ was making a statement to the "pink mafia" of porn. Like the Dred Scott Case, X-rated film performers are paid no royalties nor residuals.

And with this lack of congruence, I felt during that first endorphin-, dopamine-rich beginning of a relationship phase, I was smitten. We had our love of music to share in throw downs, alternately sharing a favorite song, discussing the performers and songwriting. EZ helped me to understand the importance of hip-hop and rap music with the voices that must be heard. We had many conversations about race, politics, travel, family, and compared notes on our peccadillos.

My Crossman DNA figured EZ could benefit by a push to advance his art. He had produced a music CD with his voice and electronics. He had a full recording studio in storage. He's had a gallery showing of his gifted photography but lacked the skill to keep a camera from breakage or loss. His photography style of reflective silhouettes is without equal.

While making my move to Francis Avenue, Aunt Jude's former apartment for the previous fourteen years, I rejected the notion of having a roommate. Too soon, too cautious, and my first lifetime opportunity to live by myself. Instead, I granted his request to store some of his belongings in my basement space. Next was a bed for him to stay here two or three nights a week, key, and use of my car.

As the sparkle of the new relationship was starting to lose luster, we took road trips on impulse. Once, we stopped at an adult video outlet in Olympia. It was there that I saw two old men get in a fight over EZ's intentions. His fame and celebrity was something that would come into play in the weirdest places.

EZ at Triangle Recreation Campground.

I started to come to my senses a couple of months in as I guided us into stage 2 of homo relationships when I said, "You know, I think with all we have in common with our tastes that I'd rather be your friend than a friend with benefits." You could call it moving more into my circle as a best friend, confessor, wingman, and protector.

EZ strikes a pose.

I asked if I could bring him along to a dinner invitation at the home of a gay couple, also close and platonic, and ready to tell me if I was making a mistake. EZ would bring his "A" game, I could not express my wonder at witnessing his witty, articulate banter that would impress, inform, and befriend in a gay culture prone to judgment and cattiness. It was that day I gave him his doctor's degree, a PhD, in life. He now was the man for all seasons. I would call him "Doc." His confidence and innate ability are evident in every social situation.

Stage 3 ensued after a while, the holidays, the court appearances for my divorce. There was a half-hearted public sale of EZ's photos, fitting the mood of the annual Fremont Solstice Festival. Ironic that this titan of X-rated films was not confident selling his art. We had a discussion about whether potential customers could take photos of his photos. It was an opportunity to speak of art marketing. Evidence of stage 3 of homo relationships started with the phrase, "Goddamn it, where are all my clean socks?" and "Stay off my computer" to "Why don't you put gas in the car when you use it?"

EZ would drift in and out of life experiences. I saw opportunities to expand his artistic expression and music. There was always hope by those of us older mentor friends of his that he'd harness the possibility of his innate talents. Stage 4, the relationship clearly has transactions and familial connotations. I would say, like some smartass, "I'd like to introduce you to my son, EZ."

EZ was quick to call me a "starfucker" when I would preface any introductions with bragging of his artistic prowess. He made it clear that it was not my "right." We did reach a point where conflicts arrived at our feet, and arguments could be fiery and explosive but for only ten minutes or so. But it has been our mutual need to get back to the BFF (best friends forever) equilibrium.

I started my own personal development journey by volunteering to tutor at Literacy Source here in Fremont. EZ followed my lead and started taking classes to attain his GED. He was impressed with himself at how his skill set made it within reach. It could have been attained if it weren't for test anxiety, and the complete overhaul of the GED exam system. And if it weren't for that wrinkle some of us have in our psyches that causes us to get close to success but self-sabotage the efforts consciously or unconsciously.

Sample of EZ's silhouette reflective photography.

Eventually, I grew fatigued of EZ's nondevelopment yet have valued his friendship in the evolutionary path of our respective trajectories of personal growth. It was time, and the signs were all there for him to move his stuff out of my basement. I was reaching the firm reality that by helping, I was codependent to his spinning wheels.

EZ always spoke of his internal goals he wanted to reach by age forty. Having had a rough forties decade myself, I cautioned him on the male midlife crisis, of life, career, and being midway in the journey. EZ would assure me he was immune to that kind of doldrums that could be titled, "I'm not where I want to be at age forty."

EZ and I remain best of friends. We have friends, acquaintances, and peccadillos in common. He dabbles in his music and photography. The porn, he's been turning down any chance at a film comeback. He is still recognized around the city. I cannot connect the dots from my friend to the man on the screen when I might pull out some porn, but I admire his courage to do the movies in the first place. He's a fixture at the table for my family holidays and rites of passage.

EZ has a respectable body of work. It's art and expression. EZ's art personified. He's like a comet speeding through our galaxy, my solar system, but more a friend today than ever. I can always call on him for help. Fremont will just have to wait to see all his talents.

I fully expect some time to see him

Onstage as a lead or character actor;

A hip-hop rapper in a homophobic genre;

With a gallery showing of his reflective silhouette photography;

A video/film director;

As a counselor, mentor to young men of color;

As a caretaker to the elderly that he so much appreciates and understands;

A thug when the situation demands it;

As a lead player to us, supportive cast members in the lives of the few of us who call him a friend;

A phoenix that rises in the many colors of the spectrum;

And to his friends and those who know him, we are spectators to his extraordinary aura that flashes neon.

Dizzy Busking Guitars

It's Dizzy at the door, his face bloodied. He looks different, in a daze.

Dizzy's a busker, a humbled street musician, open guitar case and cardboard message with print easy enough to read a safe distance from the front doors of high-traffic businesses here in Fremont. He'll play his guitars, both acoustic and amplified. I let him store his guitars and battery-powered Roland amplifier, which are his tools of the trade, under my front stairs.

Dizzy's an addict, or *a dick* as some might say. We've forged a friendship around our similar loves of music. Whether it's the stuff of the 1980s like ELO (Electric Light Orchestra), Paul Simon, Leon Russell, or the Joni Mitchell seventy-fifth birthday concert, we both admire good guitar work, honest lyrics, and songs with life's development in the melody.

A trained welder, he's a former rocker in an eighties glam era band with a lead singer who had big red dimples pasted on each cheek.

He admits to being raised by wolves. Now, fifty-seven, you can see gaps in his development.

As a child, Dizzy, born in San Diego, was showcased as one of the top 5 or so people in the United States with ADHD, attention deficit hyperactivity disorder. Today, he's replete with all the scars, gratitude, and procurement skills as an unintended consequence with learned skills. His memory is legendary; he remembers every detail.

Homeless now for several years, he describes his "Job One" is waking up each day and taking all his energy to search for that first fix.

It leaves little time to hold down a job and have significant relationships and a family. He's gone "cold turkey" for extended periods to count on his fingers. I can tell as I see a much more "together" person, more articulate, more worldly. Cross your fingers, he's been clean almost a month now.

Isn't ADHD, for some, just an excuse for bad parenting really creative children who like to multitask and, subsequently, an excuse to prescribe and sell drugs that subdue that nature or expand it? He describes that as a perfect breeding ground for full-blown addictive tendencies well into adulthood. Over the years, he has had his setbacks and fell back into that "hole." I encourage verbally but shake my head silently. I can be a friend, a daily contact, a conscience but not codependent to his deconstructed destructives.

No mean bones and no mean streaks are seen. He is full of self-awareness and self-deprecation. In Dizzy's medium-male frame, he could easily be your best employee on his good days and an ass on the bad ones.

Dizzy gets the bleeding to stop and cleans up the blood on my front steps before agreeing to step into my living room. Out of ice in my refrigerator freezer, I make up a cold compress using a six-pack of frozen sausages. He cleans up the blood from the floor.

On this occasion, he was headed to the PCC Market to busk with a stopover at Ronnie's motor home parked anywhere near here. While sitting and visiting, someone asked to try their hand on his guitar. The perpetrator cold-cocked him just once with a punch, and then his guitar was stolen. Clearly, it was assault with a witness or two. He walked away.

Looking down staircase of the Old Fremont Hotel.

This friendship is certainly not all one-sided. Dizzy is straight and suffers the taunts from his community for befriending me, a gay man. I like to trust before making a judgment. He told me early on that he'd never steal from me. A few months ago, he was nervously pacing in the yard and could not contain himself nor his self-loathing and had to come clean with the truth of getting three twenty-dollar bills from my pocket in a pair of pants hanging while using my bathroom. Subsequently, I don't trust very much, count beers, cigarettes, sodas, prescription, razors, batteries, propane, and socks.

A pivotal turning point in his young life was being sent to live with his aunt and uncle in Florida after issuing his junior high school an extortion plot and bomb threat while in eighth grade. In Florida, he was given piano lessons, which increased his mental focus.

He's got a prison record with a career in hoodlum hijinks. He credits his musical knowledge for helping him to skip a lot of violence behind bars while allowing him to hide behind the guitar in social situations. He started a prison band, which built confidence, set goals, and proved himself enough to the powers that be to get him early release.

Recently, the prospect of an additional prison sentence loomed several months on his mind. While busking in front of the PCC Market, with electric guitar and amplifier, not everybody enjoyed his sound, especially one guy, a resident in the apartments above, who came down mad and created a stir. Dizzy reacted to the assault with his microphone and cord that subsequently caused the angry guy to lose an ear. So much for no mean bones in his body.

The mad guy was released, and Dizzy went to jail. The charge was assault. The mad guy threw the first punch, but Dizzy's own court-appointed legal counsel didn't believe that one. He got another friend's recommendation for a defense lawyer who found and received the testimony of the witness who corroborated the story. Relieved, the case was dropped. Not exactly cause to celebrate but a chance to return to the status quo: homeless, music, drugs, odd jobs for same-day cash, and busking.

Sure, there are boundary issues. We struggle to maintain, despite an encroaching fulfillment of basic needs he has, and I could offer, agree to, rescue from, and enable in some quagmire of codependency. I struggle, ignore, avoid confrontation, and protect our dignity.

While I'm far from feeling the do-gooder, I question, internally and with him, if I'm helping him to gain, keep, and live independently or enabling the maintained set of norms we've established. Giving him a space to store his tools of the trade, a place to charge his cell phone, provide internet, take my cast-offs, eat my leftovers, help transport him and his belongings when he leaves one tent encampment, empty house squat, or court appointment.

Sure, there's some hesitancy and associated guilt on my part with the cold winter nights he must endure. I'm helping him to get a leg up, or so I keep telling myself that. Connecting to the many new service providers to the homeless community's phenomenon seems to fall on deaf ears. He still hangs onto the badge of independence, live by his own rules, not theirs.

I ask Dizzy regularly what are his immediate and long-range goals and where are we going with this? He says he wants to join a good band, likely old rockers with some element of name recognition, and tour Europe. For that, he needs to be clean and sober. Ironically, he'll turn up at my door at the most opportune times like when I'm just finishing preparing or eating a meal and missing when I could use an extra hand.

At times, it feels like he's on the payroll, but he's much more sensitive than I. He picks up my signals of being engaged or approaching my limit by his presence.

I haven't seen him now for about a week. I blew up at picking up the garbage and dust clouds of litter that seem to follow him everywhere like Pigpen in the *Peanuts* cartoons.

The life of a homeless man or lack of home today in Seattle is maintaining a "squat" in one of the myriad structures in the city that are vacant and awaiting demolition so that population density can be increased to accommodate all the new residents arriving every day.

Always on alert for a raid by police and usually ready to move at a moment's notice, he gathers up a few belongings, discards the rest, and puts out the drumbeat and smoke signals to find a new address.

Recently, Dizzy stopped by to charge his phone. He said he couldn't stay long because he had his old girlfriend, Kat, with him on the street waiting. I jumped at the chance to see her again and pressed him to invite her in. It was time for me to act like the grown-up after our falling out she and I had three years ago.

I began to tell her about Dizzy playing rock guitar at my annual Solstice Parade barbecue entertaining my guests. We had a pleasant visit and some wine, and her story emerged as a result.

Kat

Kat as in Katherine.

Kat as in Cat Cool.

Kat as in cathartic, as in excised demons and South Pole cold.

Kat as in catatonia, a place no one should be.

Kat as in Katmandu, and she does.

At the Speed Queen Laundromat on Francis Avenue, I got to witness all kinds of human behavior. The Clothing Exchange "Give One, Get One" is all the sign said. Some honored the sign's intent. Some tried to work some angle to their benefit. Some ignored it and just got and others just gave. And there was Kat, the customer who gave it a life of its own.

Signage at Speed Queen Laundromat for the Clothing Exchange.

And that is how I met Kat, short for Katherine. She grew up on Vashon Island from parents who raised her with middle-class values and lots of love. I finally bumped into the person who left dozens of expensive custom-made jackets, skirts, coats, high heels at the exchange. Each day, her donations would be snatched up, creating quite a stir among the other customers. Kat was shorter, petite, compact, and athletic. Her Irish ethnicity was revealed through her piercing blue eyes, auburn hair, and demeanor. She could be demure, and she could be assertive and powerful. "A forty-year-old in a twenty-six-year old's body." She was a track-and-field star in high school. Her postsecondary education was a degree in blacksmithing at South Sound Community College. A big heart for animals and people helped define her.

Kat was my friend Dizzy's girlfriend. Later, I learned this as Dizzy and Kat's belongings were being left on the street during their eviction from the room upstairs in the old Fremont Hotel Building on Francis Avenue. Dizzy was in a band with some fame but no royalties today. The eviction caused one of many breakups between them and started a four-year homeless or *sans maison* period in their respective lives.

Moses, the landlord, famous for giving everyone a break, had had enough of their antics. Kat was whatever you call them, a prostitute, hooker, call girl, or crack whore. Both were and will always be self-identifying addicts. She was a confident interloper and big-hearted, well-spoken spark plug peach of a gal. She wore her electricity on the inside but with claws ready to pounce at any insecurity or threat.

I've come to realize that to the degree a person is controlling, they are insecure almost to the same degree. Today, Dizzy rolls his eyes in relief as their relationship played out from some of the promises not kept and retaliations well set up. He and Kat have had many makeups and breakups. I've always leaned toward the left of this with philosophy finding myself too compliant, too easy to say yes, too eager to please, control balanced with freedom of choice and will. Kat admits hers is a world about control. She does the control or the relenting. Either is left to the other.

Dizzy and Kat were flop mates and squat mates from their journeys from the Fremont Hotel room to vacant houses left to the wrecking ball. Then the houses were torn down to be replaced by four-to-a-lot town houses and apartments without parking spaces in the recent building boom. Being ousted was one constant whenever and wherever they set up camp. Dizzy continued to struggle with his addiction, and I heard through him that Kat was arrested a few months later in a case involving two stolen cars and firearms. She would serve a three-year prison term at the Washington State Women's Correctional Facility in Purdy after a lengthy conviction and trial process.

Oh, that snappy, designer wardrobe Kat donated to the Speed Queen Clothing Exchange, she first told me she had a job in a business that required her to dress in power suits. In reality, it was all a costume to her escort persona. Instead of men in suits, Kat was a crack whore feeding her own dinosaur brain while being a woman in power suits to a swamp full of discerning and sharkish clients.

Kat revealed her molestation as a young girl. Her grandmother took her as an innocent young girl and her younger brother to horse riding lessons from some retired guy. With forced appreciation to her grandma paying the bill either clueless or compliant, she was repeatedly molested. She had no protectors and had a mom and dad blind to the crimes of theft to her innocence. She still has a recurring dream of herself, with her brother, trying to save her grandmother drowning beneath the ice in a frozen lake. Today she interprets that what she didn't know but knew, and was blind then to the signs, that her brother was also molested by this monster. The universe served the first blow to her trust. Later, her two older brothers got a thrill from getting this low esteem Irish-Catholic suburban teen princess high and drunk for the laughs.

At age fifteen, the very first love of her life, a schoolmate, fellow Catholic, future fraternity brothers trading booze for brains would rape her. Kat's trust, self-concept, and worldview would suffer a second blow.

Kat tells the story of how she entered her young adult life as the young bride of the black sheep husband from an old-money family. For ten years, she was married to "Boo." They settled on Maui after seeing the world on his family's private yacht that took her to Aruba,

Turkey, Syria, Lebanon, Egypt, India, and Vietnam. Boo was Jewish, and she is Irish-Catholic. She had built in two thousand years of finger-pointing religious-cultural bias to overcome with this union. Kat has the beautiful handwriting learned in Catholic schools taught by stern, pissed-off nuns. I surmise a smattering of guilt laced into every lesson.

Her marriage was idyllic, according to Kat. She must have come to that conclusion wearing rose-tinted eyewear, avoidance, or selective memory. When she met Boo, she was not aware of his wealth. He just looked like a muscled, tattooed rock and roller. After ten years on the island of Maui, they grew apart. Boo with island fever and wanting to leave. Kat was friends with everyone in town. She put down roots there with her coffee stop and landscaping business. Kat wanted to stay on Maui. The tropical climate brought out the sex addict in her despite a mutual desire to end the marriage in what she perceived as a peaceful ending. She knew by this time that she was damaged goods while trying to reach adulthood.

The day after their divorce was final in Hawaii, in a suspicious turn of events, Kat was violently raped, beaten, and set on fire by a "stalker." He killed her beloved dog. In the middle of the theft to her self-being, she was peppered with questions the perpetrator would only know to ask by reading her diary. Her best girlfriend was also raped that night in a separate location. It was now she started using crack cocaine and crystal meth, and addiction took its grip. Maui local law enforcement was oblivious to the crimes. She was a tourist *haole* anyway. My bet is it was the ex-husband and maybe his family's influence that kept these crimes from investigation or justice.

Again, the universe dealt her a third and most heinous blow to her psyche and trust and creates a tortured soul carrying way too many demons. Her personal ledger of this life and karma quotient was in the negative numbers. None of us could ever approach the level of understanding needed to fathom her three times in hell. You take a vibrant young woman with a hunger for life and knock her to the ground so far that she could never stand up fully erect again. She worries about her parents and the disappointment she's caused them. Sadness and concern trump disappointment in my parenting handbook, I try to blindly, ignorantly console her by trying to paint a hopeful outlook.

She returned home to the Seattle area and has, in her own words, "never looked back." She met Dizzy while staying in a Wallingford Motel en route to her parent's home on Vashon Island. Dizzy was a welder by day and guitar player and heroin addict by night.

Today, after five homeless years, Dizzy has a benefactor and a permanent squat in Fremont to live in if he follows the rules: no drugs and no visitors. He's had opportunity handed to him with three recording sessions provided by a studio that is across the street and used by Pearl Jam and Dave Matthews, free of charge. He makes his own music and is getting local gigs. He's clean now, we can hope.

Kat is still struggling with her lifestyle being a hooker, the drugs, and commitment to counseling as treatment. The three years of incarceration brought rehabilitation, recognition, humiliation, and a humbling. She's living in a nice squat when she's not spending time with her parents. She still sees her "regulars," especially the kinksters. She lives with some security by telling me, "I feel better about knowing that if I need a hundred bucks, I can make it, earn it anytime." She's thoughtful, caring, and kind to others but still not true to herself, and that self-actualization level of consciousness seems pretty much unattainable now without divine intervention. Dizzy recalls when their relationship intensity was at its peak hormonally. She told him of her having intimacy with others. He says it was like she was trying to say, "Put your foot down, and then I can stop." He didn't and regrets missing the one opportunity to pull her out of the hooker hollows.

Now, at age forty-nine, Kat looks forward to her fifties and the wisdom the age brings. "Kat," I'd tell her today, "your heart is too big, your arms too long, your eyes are too bright, and your aura too hot. Let's figure out a way to face your demons and change the world. Let's arrange a meeting with Aunt Jude before we call all the angels."

Where Were You in '62? Or My Fascination with the Seattle World's Fair and How It Has Filled My Head but Not My Bank Account

My little business, '62 Seattle Collectibles. I chose the name ten years ago so that it would sit at the top of a list of other like businesses in the phone book and Fremont Chamber of Commerce Directory. As if?

After stints at Pioneer Square and Fremont Antique Malls, selling through my website that looks like a third-grader did it, I crated everything up, seven crates to be exact, safely stored above my stairway and above ground. The rest of the collection hangs on my walls in what would be described as a "reluctant studio" on Francis Avenue.

I have been pleasantly relevant in my own mind with 2,800 members in my Facebook group "Seattle World's Fair Memories 1962." The Facebook page is pure, as close as it can be, free of gratuitous advertising, and members appreciate that.

At least once every year, I drag out all my stuff and spend a day as a vendor at the Fremont Sunday Market. I warn people not to get me too riled up about the topic, or they will suffer from my stories with a test at the end. Keeping in touch with the market is a way to assess the worthiness, displayability, or fashionability of memorabilia and ephemera.

I like it when I meet someone who, also at a sponge age of eight to ten in 1962, marks the fair as a milestone in their development. As schoolkids, we were filled with science kits as a reaction to Sputnik. The mood could be described as crazy giddy. My people came to the fiftieth-anniversary events clutching their souvenirs and with the chance to share stories of an event that kick-started Seattle's place on the world stage.

It's not so much about the memorabilia, but it's the city's aspirations that were admirable—to put Seattle on the world stage with confidence. Like Mickey Rooney and Judy Garland proclaiming, "Let's put on a show!" Leadership and the political climate with our Senator Magnuson, head of Appropriations, and President Kennedy taking us to the moon, the Century 21 Exposition was a perfect alignment of federal, state, and local cooperation that brought ten million visitors to the six-month fair, April 21 to October 21, 1962. Governor Albert Rosellini delivered us Elvis in the movie *It Happened at the World's Fair*.

Elvis Happened at the World's Fair.

Governor Rosellini gives a ham to Elvis; Colonel Parker looks on.

It took a lot of gall and a cheeky attitude for Seattle to pull off a vision in 1962 of the next century with thirty-eight years to go till the year 2000. The visionaries, Joe Gandy and Eddie Carlson, helped pull off the leadership for an event that likely could not be recreated today. I did just say that. Never mind. A half century had lapsed between the closing of the city's first world's fair, the Alaska-Yukon-Pacific Exposition in 1909, and the beginning of plans for the 1962 Fair. Gandy said once in 1982, "No generation—if it has any brains—is going to go through this thing twice."

The fair's legacy, the last world's fair to turn a profit in the country, left us a civic center that houses the Seattle Repertory Theater, the Seattle Opera, the Pacific Science Center, the International Fountain, and of course, the second most recognizable city symbol on earth, the Space Needle.

Portrait of 1962 *Seattle World's Fair* by E. Carpenter.

Alas, all is not Babylon, some of the seeds planted for the fair did not fully evolve: the Swiss company, Alweg, practically donated the monorail to the city with the hopes other cities would take Seattle's lead for mass transit for the twenty-first century. It eventually went bankrupt. Today, replacement parts are made in a local theater workshop.

In 1964, following the fair's success, Senators Magnuson and Jackson secured enough federal funds to expand the 1.1-mile monorail line to a 50-mile route from Everett to Tacoma. City leaders were reluctant to take on another transportation project after ripping up the middle of downtown and homes along the route to build Interstate 5. The auto industry lobby warned of an undesirable element haunting the city with public transit. Seattle declined the funds, and next in line was Atlanta, Georgia, that gladly took the chance to build MARTA.

Later, likely for nostalgia's sake, we would vote five times to build the monorail from West Seattle to Ballard. It was all but a done deal till the last vote was "no" when voters saw what it would cost them for license plate tabs. The "No" campaign was financed by downtown landlords, like now-defunct WAMU Bank, who feared the loss of downtown tenants with the obvious regentrification near each stop on the line.

The city kicked that can down the road, resulting in Seattle today, with the most traffic congestion in North America. Shortsightedness and lack of political will, with outside interests, were at play. More traffic just meant more cars and gas sold. Ballard will finally get the light rail line by 2035. I hope I live long enough.

Then there's the Washington State Pavilion, a.k.a. the Coliseum, a.k.a. Key Arena, built in 1961 for $9 million (roughly $80 million in today's dollars). Key Bank still has its name on the building but discontinued its financial connection for naming rights when the NBA Seattle Sonics left town. Now the plan is gut the building, dig a bigger hole in the ground, spend a half-billion dollars to make it look pretty for hockey, maybe even basketball. Luxury boxes and suites are needed to satiate the one-percenters among us. Amazon now has naming rights and it will be called Climate Pledge Arena.

But to be major league, the world-class city requires stadiums of stature. The Kingdome built with public funds was to be all-purpose. The concrete utility venue was ceremoniously blown to dust before we even got it paid for, making way for Safeco Field (Safeco Insurance is now owned by Liberty Mutual Insurance), and just for confusion, its new name is T-Mobile Park for baseball. For football, we have Qwest Field now called CenturyLink Field. It looks like two companies that sell air are flush to get on our lips, on our TV screens, and anxious to be one of our monthly payments and share credit for our tax dollars spent.

There's Memorial Stadium with the cries to tear it down, but it belongs to the area high schools. Again, the political forces at play and good marketing. We're spectators of winners and losers. Raising tuitions at the university is incongruent to stadium luxury boxes.

I'm asked frequently, "Why don't they have world's fairs anymore?"

"But they do," I say. "Just recently in Milan, Italy, before that in Seoul, Korea, and in 2021 Dubai."

Expo 2017 in Astana, Kazakhstan, with a future energy (without oil) theme. We just don't seem to get the invites after pulling membership in the Bureau of International Expositions in 2001. And what could be more desirable than countries sharing arts, science and technology, and culture? That leaves our military-industrial complex out of the spotlight.

And what have we done to make all these people want to move here in 2016 and 2017 and beyond? You can bet the Space Needle is included in the illustration, and the seeds were planted in 1962.

And so goes my fascination with the 1962 World's Fair, Century 21 Exposition. To me, the '62 Fair represents a metaphor for the last time this city pulled something off simply because it was a great idea.

Maybe it's just time we talked about another Seattle fair. I've got the tchotchkes for sale as a reminder from the 1909 Alaska Yukon Pacific Exposition and 1962, with a backup chorus of 2,800 poised to press their "Like" button on Facebook. Do the math. We've got plenty of stadiums, the new tunnel, light rail, museums, the arts, scientific, aeronautical, tech sectors, and Seattle is now a world-class city.

As I cautioned before we got this far, there'll be a test on your knowledge of this next time we meet.

Speed Queen Laundromat on Francis Avenue.

The Speed Queen and Me

I had the fortune and misfortune to manage the operation of the Speed Queen Laundromat just steps from my apartment and owned by my land god or landlord, as they say, Mr. Smithson, for about fourteen months in 2013. As tenants in our funky fourplex, we passed around that commitment to operate the Laundromat. Aunt Jude was managing the Laundromat when I reconnected with her in 2007. Once she inherited the million dollars and moved away, Marshall was its operator until after he retired and grew tired of the triple seven schedule. The hours were seven days a week, open 7:00 a.m., close 7:00 p.m. He moved away after fourteen years' residence here. Marshall and Bitsy had lived just on the other side of the wall-mirror-image apartment of mine in the funky fourplex. Marshall recommended to Mr. Smithson that I be next in line to the throne of the Speed Queen's kingdom. The Laundromat was small by today's standards for laundries. There were eight large stainless steel front loading Speed Queen Commercial Washers and eight companion dryers. The manager was charged with the keys. Their role in the operation involved old-school quarters to retrieve and recirculate through the changemaker machine and maintaining sixteen devices to empty daily and a soap vending machine. *Cha-ching!* Mr. Smithson would pay us by deducting our pay from our monthly rents.

Maintenance of the space occupied by Speed Queen facing Francis Avenue was straightforward. I was required to sweep the interior and exterior, scrub with Windex the exterior machine residue like soap balls, polish the stainless with Johnson's Baby Oil, empty the garbage, answer inquiries of damage to self, possessions, and machine malfunctions with my posted cell phone number as on-call resident manager. There were behavioral issues such as harassment, alcohol and drug use, petty theft of clothes, baskets, and bags. Additional duties were providing answers for missing quarters and interpreting machine instructions. Unless unforeseen smearing of lunch precipitated it, the concrete floor would be mopped at least once a week.

I added value to my role as operations manager by regularly picking up all kinds of plastic and aluminum trash, hosing puke off the sidewalk and exterior walls left from revelers the previous night, edging and mowing the slim parking strip grasses, filled with dog shit left by a pub nearby that advertises to bring their dogs inside instead of their kids. I put two large flowerpots out to accent the place, along with its lighted signage.

Funny to me this dog phenomenon in this city. If by chance you've been out to a public space and hear a baby or toddler crying loudly, you could also hear, "Shut that fuckin' kid up, will ya?" Now if it was a dog crying with a shrill voice, you'd listen to cries from the same crowd, "Oh, no, help that poor creature." "Call 911!" "Arrest that asshole owner!" Boo-hoos and indignations of what we've become as a culture when we're not looking at a little handheld screen.

Attention to detail revealed to me the secret of tidy space. The more impeccable it looked, the less litter was dumped in the first place. Clutter begets more clutter. These citizens and visitors as litterers polluters to Fremont sure reveal an irony in their behavior. Cast one's trash to the ground when no one is looking while professing to care for the environment. We have shit in this bathtub earth too much and too long before, and there are still the clueless among us.

There was my initial posture and swagger I felt I needed to exert "there's a new sheriff in town" to the denizens and characters claiming the Speed Queen as their occupied squat until caught. Friendly neighbors in this community were turned adversary so that regular customers, female, did not feel threatened while washing a few things. This was all for those who schlep their items by foot, in a car, Uber, or bus to the waters of the Speed Queen for baptism and communal dirt removal.

Besides the occupation of several homeless in the sanctum of day-to-day responsibility, there was occupation outside the laundry's doors when the weather was nice. The laundry did not have a bathroom and think of the days and ways patrons and occupiers alike relieved themselves within the business and a perimeter of 150 feet from its door. Chairs removed were dragged outside to see the daylight from the Speed Queen. Soda, beer, wine and whiskey cans, bottles, boxes were always left for evidence.

I quickly projected the scenario in my head of leaving my apartment to go to the laundry, only to have one of the street urchins take note so that access to stealing something from my apartment was possible. Or worse yet, two of them diverting my attention so that theft could occur in my home or at the laundry.

Sure, the SPD knew it well with their summonses to the Speed Queen and lower Francis Avenue. Salvador, the Bongo Man, liked to sprawl out on the sidewalk, pass out, and sleep in the sun to the degree I needed to call 911 for either SPD and the fire department truck to solve. It all depended on my situation, temperament, the operator's take on what I reported, and the weather. Neighbors remarked about Salvador and Benny, making flirtatious signals to the female customers. "Hey, good-lookin', hey, pretty lady, can you get me an OE?" was just a sampling of perceived harmless harassment.

Once, a nice-looking man with a stupid look, and who didn't look homeless, haunted the common areas of my fourplex, Caffé Ladro, the M&S Deli, (Fremart), Nectar Lounge, Kaosamai Thai, and the Photo Engravers storefront (secret recording studio for Pearl Jam and Dave Matthews). Beasley was tall dark hair with specks of gray, piercing brown eyes. We met when he had what looked to be a manufactured ploy to solicit my sympathy or pocketbook for money for a substance that dulled his senses and masked his reality. He behaved like a bipolar, split personality adolescent, though he appeared to be in his thirties. He loved to get people in trouble by telling falsehoods and tales out of school to anyone with the time to listen or care.

One day, he was repairing his bike and turned wheels over seat on the floor of the laundry. It was during Seattle's rainy season of

November until April. I quickly got in my teacher's voice, "You need to take that thing out of here, whether or not you're doing laundry." Beasley wasn't. The next day, there he was again with the bike, inside the small space, this time camped with sleeping bag rolled out. Again, I directed him for the door and made clear to take it away. It was the third day in a row, Beasley was still holding court with a couple of women customers, drinking a beer, working on the bike, tools, with tubs everywhere and smoking cigarettes. I was indignant when I raised my voice in anger, "You need to get the fuck out of here *right now!*"

Instead, he jumped up and got right in my face and said, "Nooooooooooooo!" (That's a "no" with three to four syllables.) It was then that my fight gene overrode my flight DNA for confrontation. I grabbed his shirted arms to eject this interloper in the kingdom of the Speed Queen from the premises. Fists ensued, and we took it outside to the street, where at that same instant, dispatched from another 911 incident, an SPD cruiser stopped right out front and pulled us into sequester while he responded to the first call.

I see it like it was a movie in slow motion. Out runs one of the women to the second arriving officer, and she yells "Officer, Officer, this man," (me) "assaulted this man" (Beasley) "I saw it." I guess I did produce the first hands on shoulder, but as the business' resident manager, I had to look out for the Laundromat. Missing from our walls was the faded one-page handbill produced by SPD that was titled "Conditions of Entry." Beasley volleyed the first fist. I usually just defend myself and feel like I need to get out of the web of anger like avoiding the plague, no matter who started it or sees it. Cruel Karma directed. It could have been worse, but after it was all said and done, I was self-congratulating this sixty-year-old's fragile ego on testosterone-fueled behavior.

The Seattle police officers, after taking our reports of victimhood, dismissed us to our corners. Beasley and my inflated ego self were directed and quotable to "never to speak to each other again," and "Beasley, you are never to loiter at this street, this location again." Beasley was barred from Francis Avenue for life while I drew extra points for being a resident and business operator.

The issue of the homeless came front and center with me, it challenged my assumptions, beliefs about fairness, codependency, and place. Most people just want them to go away, especially from where they live and do business. I learned early on to hand them, male and female, a buck or three just to have my back if something came down. Others of us feel we're doing them a big favor by giving money or buying a symbol they've produced for our benefit. Occasionally, proposals to do off-the-clock labor would sprout up, usually at the request of a project manager.

An opportunist do-gooder neighbor on the canal created a Homeless Facebook group and took black-and-white photos for his coffee table book. I challenged—I guess from a post he'd made, talking about buying from the homeless. I commented on the page that there were many circumstances why there's homeless. We should buy yes but not to the point of codependency or transfer of stolen goods. I was banned to "read only," no comments mode for Homelessness Emerald City. They believed it was our duty to bring out their inner beings and beauty. They did things like have an open mic at one of the restaurants. I argue for job and entrepreneurial skills.

At times, there would be unclaimed laundry for a variety of reasons and life's circumstances. I had a rack I'd found by the side of the road and mounted it with the clothes with the idea the owner might see, or likely others might take them. I posted the sign that it was a clothing exchange, "Give One, Get One." It took on a life of its own with need in mind.

Riding on the success of the Speed Queen Clothing exchange, I gathered up some magazines, books, *The Stranger* and *Seattle Weekly* free papers, and the daily *Seattle Times* newspapers for a reading exchange. More books were taken than given. Not once would anyone repair the organization their cluttering created. I took solace in the books, expanding some consciousness and perhaps to teach English, but I resented the greedy who might clear out the whole collection and leave a tattered paperback western novel in their place.

Mr. Smithson was slow to get the broken machines repaired. Then the other shoe dropped. He asked me to post a notice that the laundry would close its doors forever at the end of June. Neighbors and customers were disheartened by the loss the closing would bring. Like a community meeting place of random strangers, I'd met many interesting people on my fourteen-month stint with the Speed Queen.

Our post-Laundromatic phase of life meant taking our washable household intimates and outimates by bus, by car, or walking ten blocks uphill or ten blocks over the hill to the nearest laundry facilities. For me, it's definitely an undignified exercise I only do when I'm desperate. It's not a question of frequency—every three or four months, necessity down to no socks nor towels, desperation. Easier to buy thrift store for $1.79 and add to tonnage rather than sorting, stuffing, schlepping, *wash*, schlep, dry, fold, separate, schlep, transport, schlep, fold and sort again, hang, iron, mate, and stuff into open crevices for future use.

Before it closed, I inquired of Mr. Smithson if perhaps, I might lease the facility from him to keep it open. I did the research, consulted with my son, determined the cost of repairs, machine replacement, water, gas, and electricity, past income in quarters, taxes, and my time. We couldn't reconcile that it would produce a profit and backed out on our interests.

I staved off death to the Queen for an additional month, and the decision was made to close the doors on August 1 forever.

Like picking over the bones of a dead animal, the laundry was dismantled, and all parts and fixtures were sold off to a variety of practical types or sentimentalists to the laundry and its place in their lives.

Charlie: The Chicken Man

I always knew when Charlie the Chicken man had been in the Speed Queen Laundromat. I was resident manager. There was a residual smell that seems to come after time and after they've spent time. The scent is a concoction of boozy, armpitty, musty, musky, smelly feet, farts, bad breath, and hormones-to-go. Other times, I would catch him early morning curled up on the concrete floor in a fetal position, sleeping.

Those days, I learned a lot about homelessness, their plights, and proclivities. Charlie was a slender auburn-haired, brown-eyed man in his late thirties with an impish aristocratic-looking face, a nose like a beak in the center of a tangle of curly shoulder-length locks. Shoes and coats were elusive for the Chicken Man, as I'd see him without either or both most times on the street or in one of the many businesses here in Fremont. His never having the cause to do laundry made me get in manager mode, do my job, and expel him out into the hot or cold or wet or dry night or day.

One day, what I labeled later the "professor persona" came out of him. Charlie got my attention when he told me he had been a professor at Princeton and now was in the Seattle area and doing the street gig as a research study.

Walking back home, he approached with a quick step toward me and got right up in my face and said, "I know what you've been doing, and you are high right now!" I then thought with risk, reservation, and decided that I'd become a magnanimous, ally-building neighbor. He followed me to my living room and took a seat.

I asked if he wanted to smoke a joint. I witnessed his eyeballs moving to the back of his head in a manner searching for a response. Then he produced a few head ticks with swallows of air. His demeanor took a visible change. Charlie, the Chicken Man, was checking with the others in his head. Like it was an internal resident group meeting between his ears, seeking consensus if he could join me in passing the pre-roll sativa.

I then was startled, disgusted to almost sick at the sight of his hands.

His long slender fingers and outside of his hands were blackish, purple to shades of red. I later learned this was the result of never bathing and his environment. Charlie's hands were his tools of survival, riddled with disease. This condition provided a resistance to illness in his exterior's environments.

Charlie, the Chicken Man, could be seen any night, doing what was needed to secure a meal. The restaurant owners and their employees were generous to him. I would see him dancing like a whirling dervish outside the clubs. He was either on his meds or off. He had an uncanny ability to be almost invisible. His body was half in this dimension and hiding out in another.

I volunteered my assessment of Charlie to the neighbors and customers, describing him as good-hearted and harmless. I would discuss him with the owners of the 7-Eleven and the Deli/Fremart. Both establishments temporarily agreed not to sell Charlie any beer or wine. Why do more altering to an altered mind? I might guess the store's employees never got the memo as the alcohol sales and the residuals continued.

Like a lizard man, he embraced the banks of the canal between the Ballard Locks and Lake Union in Lower Fremont. The water with the boats, canoe rowers, and the fish fowl were his salvation fair-weather home.

Charlie got angry and allegedly accosted Sara one fateful night. Sara was single, in her early thirties, sultry, and self-aware. She resided in one of the rooms above the Fremart with the single bathroom to share. Charlie would occasionally stow away on one of the stairways to sleep.

Sara started the next chapter with Charlie, bringing in the law and more eyes that resulted in Charlie moving back to his hometown, Boston, to his family. He subsequently was hospitalized with a diagnosis of schizophrenia. This bought him time and some medication. And like a homing "Chicken," he boomeranged back to Fremont with a weight gain, a puffiness, a glare, and no eye contact.

Charlie is gone, not to be seen or heard from for the past two years. Occasionally, you'll hear people ask. What about that skinny guy with the red hair?

God's speed to you, Charlie. Let us know the results of your research here when you're ready to publish.

Fremont's Graffiti Conundrum

The dilemma of graffiti and its interpretation as an art form is a source of constant discussion in a community that tolerates and promotes self-expression.

It isn't like this medium is something new. We human species have been doing it since we lived in caves. Graffiti says, "We *were* here! This place is *ours*! This is our *tribe*!" And like other forms of art, it is open to interpretation as to its aesthetic and value.

In Fremont, as in other quarters of the city, graffiti is tied to the establishment of turf and territory of the gangs rooted in the neighborhood's subconsciousness. Rival gangs compete. And the tagging multiplies and builds exponentially if left to its own devices.

Until recently, blank walls were the canvas. Now everything that doesn't move on its own is fair to use the spray paint medium. Business storefronts, United States Postal Service mailboxes, and existing public art are now fair game.

I must say, I've never seen one of these graffiti taggers doing their handiwork, never! It is as if the artist is invisible, and the artform *is* the artist. Their canvas isn't a canvas but space on fences, walls, billboards, dumpsters, handrails, buses, trains, planes, and automobiles.

With a lot of cognitive dissonance and reluctance, I've attempted to communicate this message to my neighbors, fellow denizens, and business owners. One multiple site business owner, after repeated warnings by me and others, decided it would fit the character of our neighborhood to leave the tagging handiwork as an expression of our tolerance and promotion of our values. After three months, a gunfight broke out late one night as a likely manifestation destiny.

Ever come across or notice the sight of a pair of shoes tied together and dangling on a power line? It is a sign that there are new inductees "jumped" into the gang's membership.

There are only three choices to respond with here to this primitive art form:

1. Tolerate it. Let it flourish.
2. Decimate it. Make it look like it was never here. Let the abatement industry grow.
3. Search for common ground that accommodates the art, the medium, and the artist while accommodating the values of the neighborhood.

Is *this* art, or is it the destruction of property? Let's just leave that answer for the ages to decide.

The Art, the Artists, and the Clown

It is hard to take one seriously living in Fremont; it is the kind of place that continually reveals itself visually and in subtle ways. Artistic expression is tolerated and comes in many forms. Sure, there are the most notable installations like the *Troll* beneath the George Washington Bridge, the *Statue of Lenin* with its controversy, and the *Rocket* with its lights beneath the Saturn Building, and of course, *Waiting for the Interurban* with the glum gray transit riders by sculptor Richard Beyers.

Venture over to the Foundry building near Thirty-Sixth and Phinney, and you see another of Beyer's works carved into the concrete east wall, *Trial of Reynard the Fox*. The work covers the three-story building silently and without much notice, depicting many figures in the fable that pokes fun at the aristocracy of AD 1050. Taggers can't leave it alone. If they only knew the story behind Reynard the Fox.

There's the human figure with wings sitting on the edge of the four-story apartment building, and under a large erratic boulder are the Wicked Witch's boots as the only remains.

There are some ninety known art installations in the center of the universe, and that doesn't include those that perform their art on any given night at one of the many clubs and venues.

On this day, July 22, I pull up my Facebook account and discover it is the fifth anniversary of the death of Julius Pierpont Patches, or J. P. Patches the Clown. With a friend who's new in town, we walk toward Thirty-Fourth Avenue, which has the official street name J. P.

Patches Place. We make our way past the *Waiting for the Interurban* riders to the statue *Late for the Interurban*, which depicts beloved local children's television hosts J. P. and his sidekick Gertrude, arms locked in opposite directions, along with the ICU2TV and the Raggedy Ann doll, Esmerelda.

Late for the Interurban statues of J. P. Patches and Gertrude.

The *J. P. Patches* show was the longest-running local kid's television show in the country from 1958 until 1982. Many would say his sense of humor raised a generation or more of kids from all over Western Washington.

I must admit I was raised by J. P. In 1958, I was lucky enough to be tuned into his very first broadcast in 1958 at age seven. My parents were too busy running their tavern in Tacoma, and J. P. and his show was my constant. He was on before school and after school Monday through Friday. Unlike my biological parents, he greeted me each morning and each evening from Channel 7's studios with all the love and laughter I needed to get by.

My friend and I walk across J. P. Patches Place and pay our respects. I show him my paver stone near the base of the statue with my name and my grandson's name engraved. A man is seated at the foot of the figure, holding a bouquet of flowers. He's another "Patches Pal" there to also mark the occasion. We laugh and share memories of a simpler life in a simpler time, at least one that made more sense.

I gather up all my pocket change to deposit one coin at a time in the large can atop the ICU2TV. Proceeds go to J. P.'s favorite charity, Seattle Children's Hospital. It's a small gesture on my part and a must-do every time I visit. I know it's not legal, but I sure wouldn't mind if my ashes were left at this spot. I shed more tears, mourning J. P.'s death than my own father's. And like the clown's spirit, it is funny and a little sad, but I'm proud to admit.

J. P. Patches collage, statue, paver stones, unveiling.

We make our way back to Francis Avenue, walking uphill between the support towers for the George Washington Bridge. This *Hall of Giants* leads us to the *Troll*, which resides under the north end of the bridge. The huge troll that consumes a real, concrete-encased Volkswagen Beetle is a first in many ways and Seattle's second most popular tourist attraction. It was a first for being a public-private partnership, interactive in which it welcomes climbers to its broad shoulders, and the start of a neighborhood urban village renewal. The subsequent formation of the Fremont Arts Council has helped give Fremont its character and with adult supervision.

We head west from the troll past the Masonic Temple and Oddfellow's Hall. Both buildings serve as artifacts to a time when civic and fraternal organizations were pillars in our social structure for inclusion and exclusion. We learned norms of behavior, decorum, generosity, and service to others delivered in true tribal form. Today, we just scratch our heads and can't decide to move the clock forward or backward on our personal handheld devices.

We finish up our impromptu walking tour at the foot of the Lenin Statue. The Russian Communist leader's likeness is in exile here, the center of the universe. His presence, with the bloodred paint on his fingers, a continuous challenge to erase, creates quite a dust-up and, like good art, evokes emotion from the observer. In true capitalistic form, the statue has always been for sale after it was transported here from somewhere after the fall of Russian communism. Today, Lenin shares the stage with our TV clown. My friend now wants to live here and become a Fremonster.

Fremont's spirit is evolving with its encouragement of artistic expression. Many of the "old hippies" that reinvented this place are aging out of the civic discourse. In its place are young professionals, artists, musicians, business owners, service workers, and "characters" that contribute to the fabric that makes this place unique in so many ways. But don't just take my word for it, nor think it's all a Chamber of Commerce selling of a brand or just another tourist destination. You decide after reading some of our stories.

Millennial Monument
to Digital Divinity

Mural artist Jacobson with his self-portrait on Francis Avenue.

It's one of those things learned, I guess, by being part of a community. This one at the foot, or big toe to get more specific, of Francis Avenue. On the east-facing wall of the Nectar Lounge, formerly the home of the Baby Diaper Service laundry, was a perfectly vital but unclear theme mural. That's why it surprised me when an intense tall man with aqua-blue hair approached me while I was watering the petunias out front of the funky fourplex sidewalk. Right hand extended, friendly smiles, he says, "I thought I'd introduce myself as you're going to get tired of looking at me, staring back at you from across the street." His name is "Jacobson. That's with an O."

"Huh?" I say.

Jacobson tells me he's rented the equipment, his friends visiting were to be co-creators of a mural, but since he's now solo artist, he's doing a self-portrait, a new mural to cover the first mural.

"I'm about showing postinternet hyperrealism," he says. "By postinternet, I mean there was the invention of the internet, and everything after is postinternet."

"Yes," I concur. "It opens the floodgates as we embrace technology without fully thinking through its effect on society."

I pose a burning question. "Do we really think technology is making our lives easier? It's a catch-up game that is causing the merry-go-round to go around at a faster clip."

We must decide how much is too much technology, and do we lead, follow, or get out of the way with each innovation? I'm choosing to be a late bloomer dragging my feet, focus on function over form. The genie is out of the bottle, so the point is moot.

We're entering a time where there are dimensions of time quid quo pro at quantum lengths. And widths are our tools. It's more significant than the invention of the printing press, this internet. We're standing each day at the threshold that can reform or destroy or assist us with each decision.

He shows me his markup photo as his canvas. "It's a picture, me, facing a computer screen," Jacobson enlightens me. "There's a sense of wonder and possibility, danger and unknown, fortune and folly. Dead spaces put life into public art that should be accessible and free, and walls hold a lot of energy as does this one brick by brick.

"I'm doing some work for Jed Smithson, the club owner. I designed and painted his room upstairs."

"What's your medium, son?" I ask.

"Acrylic, spray paint with nozzles, and it'll take me thirty to forty hours to complete, and I'll put it up on Instagram and Facebook."

I think to myself that it's "postinternet hyperrealism"—that's hyperreal hyperbole.

Jacobson's combining skill sets and investing in worthwhile endeavors after a year's study at the Art Institute of Seattle. I apologize if he has any student loan debt, my generation's theft from his generation of millennials. I decide to zip it on the political statements and get right to the heart of what he's saying in the piece.

He loops back again to postinternet reality. "By his character considering the screen means nothing satirical but creates honest awareness. Art like this emits and evokes energy, to this time, this place."

"So it's not rocket science, but it does mine emotions," I wax on. "Emotions that are like a heart-tugging goodbye, infused by tears and hug induced."

The self-portrait is titled *Digital Divinity*. It projects power and potential. There is atomized paint and airbrush dark to light rendering with aqua accents, just like Jacobson's aqua hair.

Gone are the brush strokes; here are the spray cans and nozzles. Graffiti spray cans, painters, and taggers also produce today's mural art. It's just a little more real, more powerful, and by permission,

Monument to *Digital Divinity* by Jacobson.

Jacobson is a self-identified member of the millennial generation. This new millennial monument captures the millennial dilemmas and conundrums of postinternet realities in real-time serenades and not a hair out of place in the space or on the face. The face is that of a larger-than-life, one-story-tall head, warrior listening, deciding, weighing, the postinternet threshold before them. Is it people? Is it the earth? Is it human? Is it fair? Is it right? Will the mural be permanent or semitemporary?

"You know you're in the Artist's Republic of Fremont or ARF?" I ask, like he should know better.

"Yes," he says, "but I didn't know that's what they called it."

Today my own medium ironically is semigloss gray stairs paint with added sand for traction. I'm painting the two sets of stairs that face the street to the half-story walk-ups in the fourplex. My tool is a hefty four-inch-wide brush that slops and snorts up the paint. Quite a contrast defining the foot of Francis Avenue, or is this the face of Francis Avenue? I see this wondrous soul's face emitting energy as inspiration and me looking over my shoulder multitasking my realities and time dimensions, which are counterintuitive or complementary to Jacobson's.

From Jacobson on Facebook:

> New Wall, Secret Location, Non-Commercial. This one is called 'Digital Divinity' and is a post-internet depiction of our new age spirituality in the context of (Seattle) the world's hub for augmented reality and computer technology.

Its message needs to be ethereal like this—that's the only way to get people to think for themselves and not for others.

Put it in the context of what this says to the legions of folks moving here at the rate of 1,100 new residents a month, clogging the streets, driving housing prices into the stratosphere. It says, "You're here, have a vision, make the best of it," he tells me. Egos are pacified today. There's not a wrinkle in the self-esteem house of cards.

Jacobson did pick up some essential skills many artists avoid or neglect. He wants people to know he's for hire to paint.

Me, I don't think I'll tire of seeing his face as I will walk by most days and see his mug gazing back. He's an artist worthy of note for the postinternet reality with something important to say to his fellow millennials and Fremonsters like me. Two more art installations have occurred in our location. *Charms* is another spray can artist, has plans for another mural across the street, and it's time to redo the painting on the Photo Engraver's storefront with the recording studio inside. It's a chain reaction of community serving community.

Bird in center of the universe by artist, *Charms.*

The Ghosts at Home

Yep, where I live at the foot of Francis Avenue in Fremont, it's haunted. Maybe "haunted" is too severe and scary term. How about "multidimensionally occupied?" I can understand why the spirits remain here in the center of the universe. There's music, community, art, expression, and courage here.

It kind of started when Aunt Jude told me a few of her experiences as a hospice nurse, or more realistically termed midwife to the dying. I have no doubt when she has consult demeanor that she quite capably ushered hundreds of souls to their next life. She lived here for fourteen years, departing from Fremont in 2011, after the death of her two remaining brothers. I followed her and have lived here on Francis for the past eight years.

Jude startled me one night on the phone with the story of grabbing the flailing body of a young man suffering an untimely death. As she held his shoulders from behind, there was an electrical flash. She was standing on the precipice, a cliff. Beyond, she was bathed in the white light and the universe.

Just a few days ago, after a manageable dormant period, I was in the living room on the couch watching TV and heard a "ker-thump" sound. The electric circular floor buffer I had stored way up in the stairway closet, packed head up in a short box, was in the hallway in the same position as if to say, "I'm still here!" I took it as a sign for introspection about my good roommate behaviors.

After first moving into this one quarter of a fourplex, I first felt a vacuous presence when standing between the kitchen sink and apartment size gas stove. The kitchen is in the rear corner of the studio, ancient by today's standards, single sink, hot, and cold. The counters are very low as if to accommodate someone five feet tall or less. Standing there evokes a vertical vortex feeling. Bitsy, the next-door neighbor who later moved to Carnation, said she's always felt a presence when here. She's the one who survived jumping off the Aurora Bridge.

Just a few steps away is the Hoffner-Fisher-Harvey Funeral Home. One rarely sees funerals there. But at night, it's processing transitioning souls separated from their earthly shells. EZ, while living here, told of meeting a man at a bar. Exchanging addresses, it was determined he lived here before Aunt Jude.

"Why did you move from that great place?" EZ asked.

"I had no choice," the man said. "I contact the dead, and I had to get out of there for my own sanity and peace of mind."

When I finally got my act together and learned to keep a clean and organized kitchen, it was common to have all the cupboards doors closed, counters clean, and hear the cupboard doors come open, and something from the grocery staples fly out and hit the floor. Once, a crystal candle holder flipped. It went like an arrow toward my head.

Wannida, my Thai neighbor, to the front, didn't blink an eye when I told her of the multidimensional roommates. The next day, knowingly, she brought me a tied bundle of sage. She instructed me to light it to burn slowly and mark the perimeters of the entire studio with its smoke. All the while, conducting my authoritative self, verbalizing with clear expectations for our cohabitation. "Enough of this bullshit," I would say. "I know you're here. We must just get along." A peaceful coexistence is the goal.

Later, I realized I missed the opportunity, sage torch raised in the air, to lead my fellow dark passengers to the front door, down the steps, and with a shooing of my hands and say, "It's time for you to go. Goodbye!" I still have the sage torch, and if things ramp up, I'm ready to confront again.

On two separate occasions, my music system, with megawatts and speakers from the Goodwill, gave signs of tampering or a message. With my music played loud, I know the neighbors are kind to tolerate. To keep it under a riot's pitch, I never turn the large volume knob above forty on the dial. Once while downstairs in the jungle room and once while watering the garden in the back of the building, I heard loud music and quickly discovered it was my system making the walls take on a heartbeat thump. Both occasions found that volume knob dialed up to seventy while I was home alone. These were seminal moments in my adjusting to realities. Deal with it, I do. It is like a front-row seat with a window on the worlds.

I first visited the funky fourplex when I reunited after nearly fifty years with Aunt Jude in the early part of the century. It's close to Nectar Lounge that emits a beat and melody of bands on the way up or the way down the ladder of popularity. Almost nightly, a band's bus takes up a good part of the street while lounge lizards stand in reverie at their musical altar.

This is a bohemian setting with old hippies and young hipsters, performance artists, the wayward, and the homeless. On any given night, it's the part of Fremont with a pulse. After eight years, I guess I've acclimated to the rhythm of this place that celebrates, tolerates, and expectorates human expression.

I share the 1908 Victorian fourplex. The structure was moved from the route taken when Interstate 5 was built. Like a town house quad lying on its side, it was placed on a concrete block foundation with basement floor and main floor, each sharing windows. The basement was untouched for forty years or so. Twice in eleven months, while here, the sewer has backed up into that space, making it a hazmat site requiring a man in the protective suit be judge and jury for a toxic mold asylum. Our building is only one of two original structures that remain on our block. Single-family homes have been replaced, giving way to density with town houses, condominiums, and apartment homes. There are more dogs than children.

My neighbors to the front operated the Kaosamai Thai Restaurant, quite well, and they did it seven days a week. Doug and Summalee were the owners. Doug suffered an untimely death with esophageal cancer and liver failure last summer. Summalee continues to operate two food trucks while her former restaurant building is now run by millennials in hoodies. They promote the bar over any food. Call it a revival, but their parking lot is now host to ax-throwing competitions. The concept never quite caught on and Summalee has the restaurant back. She had an exquisite remodel done to the space, and the regulars, like me, are glad she did return.

Wannida and her son Julian were loyal, longtime employees. They now work six days a week at another Thai restaurant here in Fremont. I share a wall with them and the other wall with a man, "Neighbor." He doesn't say anything about my ruckus habits, nor do I say anything about his. "Neighbor" from time to time, with his allergies and sensitive nose, says that he picks up odd smells. (It's likely the rabbit he keeps in a cage.)

My red door with eighteen windows is a relic from a past that made us feel more secure. The door is a half flight up, and the front stairs are all wood. There's the hazelnut tree and its fruit stolen by the squirrels every time. Three raccoons roam the yards and gardens each night in search of nutrition, and they avoid humans with nasty mean glares.

A real live spirit medium paid a visit recently. After soaking up the place, he matter-of-factly reported two spirit entities call this place home—one man and one woman. He said one of them, likely the woman, doesn't like me living here while the other does like me. I'm good for a buck donation to feed their demons, the other, likely the man, is humored by my antics.

A while back, I had a dream while sleeping in my bed quarters. I've taken lately to sleeping facedown on my stomach. Either I dreamed this, or it was performed in real time. I try to get up, lifting my head first, then my head and shoulders. It feels as if my body is covered entirely by a heavy-weighted blanket. It weighs enough that I cannot move. I struggle. Keeping my head down, I make repeated attempts to stand. I get up finally on my knees and back out of the bed. In my peripheral vision, I sense another entity. It is behind me. Standing, I turn, and it turns away only faster than me. I turn around, and it does the same no matter which direction I struggle with. Frustrated, I try to psych it out and finally face nothing but the entity. It startles me as if to give me a tickle in my belly. The spirit grabs me, and then we spin around the room as if performing a grand turn on a dance floor. This is in a dark living room.

Later that same night, I have trouble sleeping. I think about that dream. I try to make sense of what it means. I remember Aunt Jude, hospice nurse, midwife to the dying. I make a note of the funeral home just a short block away and its dark of night crematorium. I hear a creak on the floor and in the hallway by my bed. I lie still on my stomach with my right shoulder higher. A heavy weight drops on top of my back as if wedged against my right side. I hear a slight giggle, and pressure intensifies. Lying still, I gather up the internal emotion to acknowledge a presence. "I await judication," I hear. But on second thought, I think maybe they're saying "jurisdiction."

Gladys, my sister-mom, passed away three months ago after a long journey of stubborn, mean, certifiable crazy dementia. After nineteen days in the emergency room of Tacoma General Hospital, I was called to testify against her in a courtroom before a judge at Western State Hospital. There was a subsequent two months in a lockdown geriatric psych unit, she was fed drugs to break her spirit. Her passing was both loss and relief. The funeral home steps away handled the arrangements, including her cremation.

About this time, while sitting in my living room one evening, three framed pictures simultaneously jumped off the south wall and onto the floor. "Hmmm, that's weird," I say to myself. "It must be the neighbor," I think, "pounding on the walls with his head against his headboard."

An hour or so later, a large, heavy brass ship's portal wall clock on the east wall of the same room falls as if deliberately pushed and lands face down on the couch. Chills run up and down my spine, the hair on the back of my neck stands up, and I estimate if someone had been sitting under that clock, there would have been significant injury to the head below.

My imagination playing tricks on me? Or my subconscious is telling me I've got to lighten this load I've been carrying and put down the crosses I bear?

There's the garden, ever-changing as my north side gets the direct sun only in the summer. I accept it as my substitute for regular counseling sessions. It is a little urban oasis that attracts sparrows and finches that nest, and a murder of crows stationed on the wires with the charge to deliver things to the void while providing to me clumps of roof moss turds left by the front doorway. The patio square of paver stones is my expression collection of rocks I've gathered, gewgaws made of glass, and artifacts for future archaeologists to interpret life in the early 21st Century.

I can't take all the credit for the garden. Garden markers, statues, and other things just appear. The figures of the Buddha, the little girl with the bird on her arm, are volunteers. I know not from whence they came. I just smile, embrace, and marvel at the creative energy of the place with earthly and otherworldly "multidimensional occupants."

The journey has changed me, and I've changed the journey.

Nectar Nights and Other Waiting Rooms

I've been to just a few, hope to find more though, places, spaces, destinations suitable for designation as heaven's waiting room. This is truly a place where I can say to the universe, "Just let me hang out here before I move on in this earthly life." It doesn't matter what the cost, it's the spirit, the captivation of my short-attention span, shorter memory, and the "vibe."

It is deservedly a short list. In Seattle, it is first The Triple Door, a three-hundred-seat supper club. Second is Add-A-Ball, literally, a hole-in-the-wall pinball machine bar steps from home. Last is the Nectar Lounge, a nightclub less than three hundred feet from my pillow. Ironic that two of the three are right here in the center of the universe.

Fremont is a place that nurtures the spirit of the artist. It's a place that doesn't take itself too seriously.

Living here can be a contact sport. Win, lose, or tie, everyone has a story to tell about a clash between the forces of residents and the homeless, businesses and their employees and the homeless, the homeless and the homeless. Add nightly doses of midnight revelers, making the sidewalks, club's venues, and corners their stage, their canvases, soundtracks for life's expressions, dramas, comedies, absent of restraint.

Music is the ingredient that is difficult to quantify for its effects on the participant, residents, and artists who pass this way on their way *up* and their way *down* the ladders of success, fame, peace of mind, enlightenment while honing their craft. I've always admired the artists' nerve, the courage to put themselves "out there," for the rest of us to take in, enjoy, and judge. Fremont is a place that nurtures or kills that spirit.

When stars align, planets do too, and done right, it's those serendipitous moments I love. When artist, observer, participant, and the room synchronize.

A while back, I was making one of my increasingly frequent late-night walks to feed my distractions, destructions, angels, and demons on my shoulders.

As I make my way, I'm drawn in by the by a singer's voice with his acoustic guitar laid across his lap within earshot and eyeshot of the sidewalk. On warm nights, I can see performers from the sidewalk on stage at the Nectar Lounge. I've always been a sucker for the stylings of singer-songwriters. I stop long enough to sample a couple of his songs, check out his name from the playbill. He's Owen somebody with a last name, and he is only the opening act. He is opening for the Devon Allman Band.

Drawn in often to performances at Nectar, this night, I decide to plunk down $15 for a ticket to likely stand for a performance and a shot. Most nights, though, I hear it from my stoop, or from my pillow as I fall asleep, or from my couch with television remote in hand, increasing its volume that competes for my divided attention.

For once, I'm pleasantly surprised that I'm not the oldest person in the room this summer night. Looking around the very small crowd, I ask myself, "How do these old people track this club's playbill?" I feel the power of social media and the intersection of artists, listeners, and club owner's marketing savvy. Does the artist or club or audience track whom?

Maybe this baby-boomer-infiltrated small crowd are like salmon returning to mysteriously ancestral grounds, instrumental to their genetic origins. In its previous incarnation, the Nectar Lounge was the Baby Diaper Laundry service. If we follow the demographic and trending needs, both businesses cater to bodily functions and expressions. I am respectful of the relevance it bears to its place in the center of the universe.

I step in and nervously find a spot to stand unobtrusively in a room of thirty or so fellow passengers. I remember my original food-finding mission. Deciding to forego the menu at the bar in favor of a hand stamp reentry past the six-foot-eight, four-hundred-pound security man. I dash home to make and gulp down a peanut butter sandwich, lock the front door, and return for Owen somebody's opening act. He's joined on stage with the headliner's accompaniment and softened transition to a stage break. I order a whiskey "neat" (that's with no ice). Long ago, I figured I'd rather enjoy what is on stage than make frequent trips to the music venue's bathrooms.

I'm mildly amused and annoyed at a perfectly sane-looking middle-aged woman, except for the look in her eyes, storming, pacing, and chanting, "Fuck Donald Trump! Fuck Donald Trump!" while marching around the dance floor below the colorfully lit, foggy-elevated stage. The headliner, it must be, comes out again to appease her. Something must have worked; she decides to stop.

With tablet in hand, I do an internet search of tonight's band with the namesake "Devon Allman." Descriptors like "Southern Rock," "Rock Royalty," "Allman Brothers" top the list. With Uncle Duane, Father Greg, tonight is Devon's thirty-ninth birthday. Same age as my son, Ryan, whose birthday was a week earlier. I am transported to the week of Ryan's birth in memory, remembering Cher and Greg Allman's son, Elijah Blue, would be the same age. "Well, d'ya know?" I think to myself, "It *is* the son of rock royalty playing tonight." I smile to myself.

Unavoidably, I draw attention to myself with a pen and journal in hand. I journey through trademark Southern rock guitarists, trademark Allman Brothers stylings, and vocals. Those of us in this room seem to give each other that Mona Lisa-knowing, contented smile, affirming we were in for a great evening, where the present meets the past and the future or maybe we were just sitting and standing in heaven's waiting room. It feels like the band is playing right to me. It is the eye contact, the wink, nod, and smiles as they work the room. It works on us. I will wait here in a blissful, patient presence before being called to those pearly gates for processing.

The lead singer reveals his birthright guitar talents with his dark hair and prominent silhouette. I can see his mother, Cher, with his big head and tall compact-tattooed frame. I see his father, Greg Allman, with an impish, pit bull smile.

A lone couple creates the dance floor. He with his tie-dye T-shirt, and she with her jiggling moves in her long skirt and athletic shoes. The rest of us just pull out our half-smile head bob best suited to the blues look of listener appreciation.

The band plays a cover of Bob Marley's reggae, "No Woman, No Cry." I admire this older couple as they venture about the concrete floor. They dance and give each other a tender embrace. She nuzzles into her dance partner's neck and shoulder.

We feel the love and those tears that accompany one of those center of the universe synchronistic moments. And those tears are tears of joy.

Center of the Universe
Magic Moment

I pulled my car up to park a few doors up from my address on Francis Avenue. Parking is always a challenge here in Fremont. Finding a spot for the car is a roll of the dice and seems to be more so if one has a lot of groceries or laundry to carry.

There was room for three cars to park between driveways. Driving my Honda Element, a.k.a. boombox on wheels, that is too long in the back and too short in the front, not the car but likely my advancing age of declining senses at play here. I need to sidle up to the curb when I park my car. I pull up first to the furthest parking space and proceed to go in reverse down Francis until I am at the lowest parking space. I'm relieved I didn't have to parallel park on this hill.

Prior to this trip with all that had transpired, I felt obligated to drive. Taking in the Ballard Seafood Fest was my idea. I was able to hold off addressing the missing Nissan key belonging to Allan. He's my partner, nondomestic category, marvel to my family, Eagle Scout, Mr. Volleyball, the dean, and official's official. He's my complete opposite and brother of a different mother. He's there with moral support, providing solicited and unsolicited advice.

Since crowds equate to no parking options to me, I suggested riding the two bikes I have from Fremont to Ballard along the "human freeway," the Burke-Gilman Trail. Veto the bike idea! Allan is the consummate jock to the degree I'm not one. He's an avid volleyball player—a recent gold medalist in the senior games. Allan is handy. He fixes and designs and builds things. Allan is a man of deeds, where I'm a man of words. I am so full of bullshit. I stink. He's a competitor, and that makes me a communist. My ideal sports are ultimate Frisbee and pinball and Comedy Sportz at the Oddfellows.

There's an elephant in this room, and it's the issue of his car key. Well, no key actually. And this is after almost two weeks missing that key with the $400 replacement cost.

Picture a little Nissan pod with buttons about the size of a flat egg. The so-called key looks like a pair of tweezers that I insert into the pod like an arrow to a quiver. To start the car, you put your foot on the brake and push a button, and you don't even need a damn key, except maybe when I've locked it inside the car.

A couple of weeks earlier, Allan had returned from a week in Dallas officiating a National Volleyball college tournament. He dallied to my nagging about leaving for the airport in plenty of time and not raise the blood pressure or heartburn or armpit sweat and glide right into the Alaska Airlines first-class seat. Instead, he called me en route to the airport to say he would have to leave his car captive in the concrete, $30-a-day ransom charge parking garage run by the Port of Seattle.

He wanted me to drive or get myself down to the parking garage's sixteenth floor that day and pick up his car to save money. So I asked a good friend, EZ, to accompany me as we take a chunk outa the middle of the day (thirty minutes' drive each way on a good day). EZ drove my car around in circles at the Seattle-Tacoma Airport while I went to find Allan's coupé on the top floor of the parking garage. I searched and searched. The "key" to start was locked inside the car. Keyless was I, and so without the push-button for a foot on the brake pedal start. This trip was a waste of time. One more day's ransom to the port. (This is the autonomous governing body that at one time had no plans to have our light rail reach the airport to keep their lucrative parking lobby and taxis drivers happy.)

Day two, another large chunk of the day. This time, now two days later and more fees, as he FedExed the key pod with the tweezers to me. Success! Nissan retrieved! EZ drove the car back to Fremont. I drove my car with $86 spent for Nissan's ransom. We parked the car up the block for the duration of his Dallas trip. Never again, I affirmed to myself.

Over the next few days, the car was left on the street. I picked Allan up at the airport and drove my car back to his car. I gave him the tweezer key but couldn't locate the key pod with the buttons.

Several times, I was asked to return the lost pod. In the days turned to weeks that followed, I waffled, finally saying, "I dunno where the hell it is. Maybe—Let's go to Ballard Sea Food Fest!" I divert. "With the fresh barbecued wild salmon, coleslaw, and garlic bread for only $10."

My proposal bought me some time, clearly turning into an angry time. I managed one last delay and said, "Okay, let's go eat the salmon fest, and when we return here to my place, I will go through all my dirty laundry with a metal detector and borrow a drug-sniffing dog to find that pod." I looked online at what it would cost me to replace it. Hmmmmm, $400. I will find it!

I drove. I was in combat mode parking my car in Ballard. We ate. We ate, listened to the bands, and like salmon swimming upstream, we navigated the vendors, the Market Street stores, and sidewalk sales.

Time to go home. Still with me, reader? I made my left turn from Thirty-Sixth Avenue up Francis and searched for parking spaces hard to find.

And this is where the story began.

I spy three spaces up the block between two driveways. I pull my car up to the northernmost space, then back down and settle for the southernmost space. I jockey my toaster box of a car and pull up and back next to a tree. Allan is in the passenger, shotgun seat.

I say, "Look at that tree. Is that another hops tree?"

We both survey the tree, and at the same moment, without a word uttered, we notice something hanging in its branches.

It was there in that tree. There it was! It was the key pod hanging from that tree like low hanging fruit. Someone must have found the key pod. It was found at its most opportunistic timing when I was desperate. I would have returned home, dug through my dirty laundry, searched under furniture, turned over every leaf up and down the street to keep from spending $400 for its replacement and to keep my pride intact shielding myself from the "I told you sos," having my reputation besmirched and reliability questioned. Instead, I was touched by basking in the center of the universe magic moment and the wonder. Thank you! I say to this universe and those beyond.

Riding the Rails

Mitchell was a career Milwaukee Road Railroad man. And this railroad is how Mitch and I struck up acquaintances. I too was a railroad fan having a dad, two uncles, likely hired nepotistically, and a grandfather, a legendary engineer, who worked on the Milwaukee Road Railroad and died on the Milwaukee Road Railroad.

Customers had to walk down Mitch's concrete stairs to the subterranean gallery space and storefront in the supposedly reclaimed section of commercial Fremont. There used to be no reason to go there—Fremont and its 1911 bridge was eclipsed by the George Washington Memorial Bridge, better known as the Aurora Bridge, in 1932. It towers above, a full six lanes in place supported by the *Hall of Giants*. That was before the *Troll* started Fremont's trajectory to its higher self, standing for freedom of expression and the freedom to be peculiar.

Another aspect of the taller span was its magnetism for suicide jumpers, jumpers hundreds of feet from guardrail to canal and mouth of Lake Union below, to the dismay of the houseboat residencers at sea level. There's a suicide prevention fence now to keep the jumpers on the right side of the rail. Last century, there were a plethora of railroad lines building tracks hundreds of feet below. Technology made way for steam engines, electric engines, diesel engines, and coal and wood-fired engines. The rails evolved as did the region's love of cars, trucks, boats, bikes, buses to today's clogged highways and surface streets earning the city distinction for some of the worst traffic on the planet.

Fremont was even home to the Interurban's Trolley Barn and a mass transportation system that was rolled up and smoked by residents in 1941, who preferred sucking on the end of their own automobile tailpipe.

Established in 1901, the Milwaukee Road went bankrupt in 1986. The line is mostly defunct now that led from Tacoma to Chicago. Grandpa Bill Crossman died of a heart attack at the age of fifty-nine in 1960 at the controls of a locomotive coming down Snoqualmie Pass into North Bend. Mitchell had no memory of my family. That generation has now passed on. Noted, it was something Mitchell and I had in common.

Our bubbling nostalgia for the rails netted me an invite to visit him. I was a contributing writer for the *Fremocentrist* online news and saw an opportunity for a story and friendship.

Upstairs, the living quarters of Mitchell's studio was occupied by his ex-partner. They once shared the space, but it must have been an amicable split.

Mitch had set up residence in the gallery, it appeared, and was living in the office, windowless, walls lined with flags from all over the world, but in storage, an old computer, desk, desk chair, boxes of files, and a couple of folding chairs. The old kinkster slept in a sling when he wasn't using it for more carnal pleasures.

The rest of this story still puzzles me. Mitchell was near late retirement age. He clearly wanted to sell his share of the gallery for pursuit of an easier life.

After the pleasantries and flirtations, I started to feel like I had arrived to witness a train wreck of sorts, of ideas, biases, emotions, and perversities. It felt like sliding on my butt down a rabbit hole to an alternate universe, here in the center of the universe no less.

Mitchell, the railroad man, was of medium height, spotty white hair, a little thick around the middle with an authoritative deep pitch to his voice. But he had that crazed look in his eyes. I never know whether it was a good crazy, or crazy, crazy, or even under-the-surface and under-the-belt crazy.

Standing in the studio, we talked of our railroad memories, trains, and stories. We queried our list of possible common acquaintances from the old days, Fremonster to Fremonster.

But on this summer afternoon, Mitch was preoccupied. He carried on and whined on and on about a young lover of his, thirty years his junior. The gist of the jammer was when he declared, "Tom can fuck me like no one else can. He's been beaten up and was admitted to some hospital in the Tri-Cities." (Otherwise known to locals as the dry-shitties, tucked away in the southeast corner of Washington State.) "He got beat up, and he's there with *that* girl of his by his side. That bitch will ruin his life."

"How dare she get in the way!" Mitch spits in disgust. "I need to go over there and talk with him and convince him to come back here."

Trying to be helpful with my usual self-important "It's so easy problem solving when it's not my life" advice, I started to ask questions of my fellow Fremonster. I could tell he was acting out of character for a man in his early seventies. In between his pontifications that were endless, this old fart carried on and on about this guy Tom. I finally got to the point of telling him he plainly needed to give this horse up for pasture.

Mitch snapped back at me. "You don't know what you're talking about!" Dismissing me, he said several times, "It's none of your business."

"But," I pointed out, "Tom's much younger and must find his way, another life of his choosing. Just what is your claim over him? It's time to consider the campsite rule, Mitch."

"What's that?" he defensively asks.

"Just like a campsite, leave them in better shape than you found them."

"Tom and his dad live nearby," Mitch rattles me. "You know that Tom's dad fucks him too?"

"WHAT?" I say. "That's wrong, it's incest, and more wrong on so many levels of humanity."

"Well, it's okay that his dad fucks him." Mitch is in categorical twilight zone demeanor now with a sick rationalization. "The mother is sick, the dad can't have sex with her, and it's family."

Oh, Grandpa Crossman! I think. *I'm sorry your name is included in this story*!

"WRONG! WRONG! WRONG!" I tell him. I don't falter with my disgust.

Here's Tommy. He's in a hospital clear across the state with his girlfriend and trying, it appears to me, trying to make a new life.

Mitch, in full nonauthoritarian victim dazes, says, "I need to see him. I need to talk with him."

I should have ended the visit. Finally, more invested in this argument than I should have been, I try to get between Mitch's ears and eyes with my imperative: "Dude, *you* need to get a grip here and move on beyond this."

To perhaps close this manic episode, I helped Mitch find the phone number to the Tri-Cities hospital caring for Tommy. He gathered his wits and dialed the phone number, only to reach Tommy's bedside.

The girlfriend answered Tommy's phone. Tommy was sleeping, and Mitch from my one-sided end got a colder than expected reception from her. When he finally got to speak directly with Tommy, the words were frozen somewhere between Fremont and Richland.

Hanging up the phone, he looked anxious and upset.

Mitch tells me since Tommy was gone, he wanted to have sex with Tommy's dad.

"At least," I deadpan, "the dad is closer to your age and not a blood relative."

We ended the evening as we both tired of each other's company.

Mitch eventually sold his share of the gallery business.

Mitch and I met a second time on his turf. It was to shoot some photos of him for the story I was writing for the *Fremocentrist*.

This second meeting, I was met with even more of Mitch's angst toward Tommy than before. Mitch was composing a letter on his computer to mail or hand deliver to Tommy. Still in the Tri-Cities, released from the hospital, and now taking up residency.

Mitch is preoccupied as I try to tie up some loose ends for his article. "I have to talk with him, alone, without *her* in the room," he sputters without looking up from the screen. "Tommy needs to stay close by here in Fremont. It's his duty."

I roll my eyes, and I think, *Here we go…*

"Dude!" I say to get Mitch's full attention. "Give it up already. *You* have got issues. You might even need some professional help so that at least you all can come through this and out the other end whole."

He eventually slides into and through the boundaries of convention when he drops this little F-bomb, "Oh, I fucked Tommy's dad since you were here last."

"Really?" I ask like I'm expecting more.

"It was weird," Mitch says under his breath. "There were animals involved."

I'm nauseous and now in absolute disgust.

My divergent mind has a train wreck with my convergent mind: I deduct and extrapolate. Tommy was born with a fraternal twin brother, Timmy. Tommy was the alpha twin, yet the two were very different personalities. Sibling rivalry was an understatement between the two. Tim and Tom, in many ways, were opposites; one athletic the other not; one extroverted and the other introverted; and one gay and one straight.

About fifteen years ago, while in their twenties, Tim was found dead on the Milwaukee Road Railroad tracks. Investigators could not conclude whether Tim had been hit by a train or if he was murdered and his body left on those tracks. Tim's death was ruled a suicide and an accident for expediency maybe.

This visit, I laid it on thick to Mitch as I snapped photos of the Railroad Man with the missing Railroad Twins. I kept my questions flowing and my curiosity high. This was stuff Mitch didn't want to hear from a nosey neighbor like me.

Again, I pleaded with this grown man, "Dude! Get a life," I press. "Get a grip! Expand your thinking instead of contracting your thoughts."

"You need to get the hell out of here right now!" he fired off the admonition. Mitch all but chased after me with bluster and huff as he threw me off the premises, chasing me with a broom. It was the last time we spoke. I slunk home to the foot of Francis Avenue, tail between my legs.

Three days later, I still can't get the last episode out of my mind. I use my cognitive dissonance to hypothesize how the story was either fictionalized or truth-seeking.

Tommy's twin Timmy died far too young while they were both in their twenties. Mitch explained how Tommy suffered a lot of guilt at being the surviving brother. Mitch seemed selfishly determined to keep Tommy controlled. Controlling behavior is simply borne out of insecurities. Mitch, the career railroad man, the dad, and twins were longtime friends. The twins, the urgencies, the time, and the tempers interplay.

The truth could be shrouded in the legends of a bankrupt railroad company or on or under the tracks pulled up to make bike trails from Fremont to Chicago.

The truth will never be told or fully known. Tommy died last spring in a motorcycle accident at the early age of forty-seven, still in the Tri-Cities. Mitch moved into Tommy's dad's house and points elsewhere with his sculpture of a nymph he named Ramona.

My story was never published in the *Fremocentrist*, nor completed, until now.

When I ask around the neighborhood about Mitchell, Tom, Tim, Mitchell's ex-partner, the dad, I get the same answer. "Oh, *that* guy," their voice fades quietly. "Those guys."

Ramona is gone from the house now; it looks like the rest are gone too.

And our rail transportation system is fifty years too long and fifty years too late.

Me Come Gambia

Once upon a sleepless night, I discovered a Craigslist post from Literacy Source, a nongovernmental organization, in the adult workforce training education system, right down the street, just a few steps from my home. It was a call asking for volunteer tutors to work with individual students, mostly recent immigrants, who receive tuition-free classes in basic skills and citizenship. Some 250 people volunteer as tutors for those who request it.

For over two years, for two hours, two days a week, I volunteered acting like a tutor, and my charge was Ousman, then age forty-eight, newly minted United States citizen, born in the Islamic Republic of the Gambia located in the western armpit of the African continent. Ousman immigrated to Seattle, Fremont, in a marriage that some could say was convenience.

He was wait-listed at Literacy Source* almost two years prior to get assigned a tutor, me, to assist his English language development and advanced employment. As a retired educator, receiving a state pension, I felt it was a way of giving back. Well yeah, that's a good reason. Actually, I had the time. I was depressed and needed an outlet for my "teacher voice" that can bore my unwitting friends and contacts until they yawn, their eyes roll back in their head, and I've succeeded at boring them to tears. I'm trying to say I get just as much back and more from the service to my citizen charge.

---

* Literacy Source outgrew their Fremont location and relocated in Lake City with a larger site closer to the populations they serve. I continued to volunteer at Literacy Source and worked short term with several other students also recent immigrants.

Ousman had just earned his US citizenship, preparing for the tests and paperwork, and interviews with knowledge and appreciation that exceeds most natural-born citizens. His dream was to leave his job as a swing shift janitor in the Seattle Municipal Tower and with my help attain a Washington State Commercial Driver's License (CDL) to get behind the wheel of a trailered semi for the open road, and the highways, byways, and natural wonders of North America.

Hear told, Ousman's ticket to the Emerald City and residence on Fremont's Top of the Universe goes back eight years to that life-changing taxi ride in Bwiam, the Gambia. It was a Muslim holy day. A woman, also a Fremonster, could not get transportation and kept asking taxi drivers for a fare to see the Slave Memorial near the village of Bwiam. None of the male drivers would break ranks, all refusing her fare except Ousman. His upbeat resilient personality must have made an impression on her. From that point, it was a whirlwind and tornado marriage first, courtship second, *and* a pre-nup arrangement with him wild-eyed for the American dream he'd only heard about. By most indications, it was a union with expanded control and a financial upper hand in the legal and moral marriage contract. "Travel escort," did I say? Outwardly, it looked like she was some Seattle do-gooder liberal and lonely.

The first words in English he said upon arrival in Seattle before Customs and Immigration were "Me come Gambia."

In his Gambian family, Ousman was a modern man. His mother gave him her blessings before she died for his American journey. He had a strange belief in having one wife in a country that permits multiple wives, thereby rejecting the norm for a man of substance in the Islamic Republic of the Gambia.

Making a living was Ousman's primary focus in his homeland with his commercial driving positions and owning his own taxi to serve family and tourists. Illiteracy for him trumped going to school. Learning, much less writing, the storytelling language of Senegal and the Gambia, known as Wolof, was through osmosis. Ousman sent money for his niece's tuition so that she could stay in school. His brother-in-law neglected to value his daughters getting an education.

Ousman, like legions of immigrants before him, wired quickly into the network of those fresh off the boat from the African continent here in the United States and residing in Slugville (Seattle). According to Literacy Source professional staff, his new spouse and benefactor served as barrier-in-chief to his dreams of achieving a GED and US citizenship. "If you'll be my Dixie Chicken, I'll be your Tennessee Lamb, and we can walk together down in Dixie Land" (Lowell George, Little Feat).

For the right reasons, Ousman, with citizenship in hand and first-grade reading level, had one goal. He wanted to drive a commercial vehicle like a van, school bus or passenger bus, and maybe live long enough to achieve his ultimate dream to pilot an interstate, big-trailered rig in which to see the USA from behind the wheel of a sleeper cab.

For me, this retired teacher, 2011 was the year of walking depression that comes with leaving a long-term relationship. Getting up each morning and making a conscious effort to move first the left foot then right foot in the learning to walk stage of achieving personal equilibrium. Volunteering my time was like reaching into the dark, providing a helping hand to someone, pulling that hand out of the darkness to find that other hand was my own. It helped me to discontinue my wallow.

Ousman is much taller than my six feet. His lanky body, long neck, burning brown eyes make a commanding presence. We met midafternoons while he was on his way to work downtown. He usually dressed in light-blue jeans and a black windbreaker with the uniform shirt for his employment, a contractor that janitors the city of Seattle Municipal Tower.

Somehow, reading Dr. Seuss's *Cat in the Hat* looking over the shoulder might help third graders, but it wasn't going to cut it, nor in my opinion, help anyone's dignity and confidence here. Containing proper, useful English, albeit with bureaucratic legalese voice, leading to streams of blind alleys in the content, I chose the Washington State Department of Licensing Commercial Driver's Guide as my curriculum, along with basic grammar exercises and selected newsworthy and inspirational readings. He would deliver these aloud in the library of Literacy Source.

Volunteer or not, my challenge was to make each session as compelling, productive, and memorable as possible. I spoke of attaching a picture in his mind and hanging it on hooks like a filing system. I learned quickly Ousman wasn't prone to do any homework nor writing exercises. I tried to start each session with an opener warm-up. Perhaps we'd do a perusal of the transportation job posts on Craigslist. We put together his résumé. He was comfortable to stop whenever we approached words outside his knowledge base for my definitions and clarity. Along our journey as tutor and tutee, life happened too.

One day, Ousman took a phone call from his sister in the Gambia during our tutoring session.

"Jaam nga am?" he greeted her (Have you peace?). It was my first chance to hear his language in conversation. Speaking Wolof, it appeared there is little punctuation but a steady stream of rolled Rs with the jaw almost clenched and still with a peppering of French for objects and nouns.

Pronunciation through read alouds in English, long and short vowels fell into place, which led to parts of grammar differentiating nouns from verbs, adverbs from pronouns. His reading level would increase but all too slowly for my impatient nature.

Near the end of our two years together, two days a week, two hours a session, I found we could get further just by focusing on the samplers of multiple-choice CDL test questions from around the country. His reading and responding gave it a game show aspect and snapped time along with the immediate gratification of the right answers. There were times he would come to a session, and his knowledge would seem to diminish, and other days, he would build on previous knowledge and knock my socks off.

Ousman's extended family needed his help. Internet communications tools like Skype video conferencing was his way to keep in touch. It wasn't the best tool for language skill building though.

I was afraid I created a monster when showing him how to buy on eBay. He soon accumulated a collection of disparate phone parts, which led to car parts to repair Renault and Saab brand cars both in Seattle and popular in his home country.

Ousman seemed outwardly to be a high-strung person, but this was offset and overshadowed by a Zen-like calm he possesses, leaving a lasting impression. His "boys of summer" attitude was explained observing his need to clear his computer of any unwanted programs or e-mails. He meticulously made sure they were all placed in the computer's Recycle Bin. But that wasn't enough, he would circle back and make sure these items were deleted from the Recycle Bin. He could live unfettered, in the present, and anxiety-free.

An entrepreneur in the Seattle African community has an intermodal container down at the Port on Elliott Bay. For a few dollars, countrymen pay a small amount to ship objects like shoes, bicycles, car parts, generators, and solar panels to the Gambia. When the container is full here in Seattle, it is then bound for irregularly scheduled voyages home to the port near Bwiam on the River Gambia to family and enterprising individuals. Shoes from China, he reports, "barely last one day."

Ousman's sister, Haddy, needed economic independence; her husband was marrying a second wife. I helped him find a sewing machine on Craigslist. He wanted to give his sister a tool for earning income. For about a dollar US, she could have about fifteen minutes of electrical power provided by her village generator. Sometimes, the man with the gas to run that generator would bring the gas, and sometimes, he pocketed the dollar.

I admired Ousman's dedication to his learning. Middle-aged learners don't retain new knowledge as well as the younger students. Working full time and overtime janitoring the City Municipal Tower, learning English, technology, and our culture, his wife became increasing frustrated with him. He reported she would have angry bouts of emotion. She had the means and time for adventure world travel. But Ousman wanted to be better anchored here in Seattle. At his insistence, I helped him find additional jobs to fill his bank account and his time away from the home front. All the while, he kept his dignity and resolve. I suggested he network through social media for employment opportunities. He told me his wife wouldn't permit him having a Facebook account.

Eventually, the convenient marriage became inconvenient when he was kicked out of his home one Saturday. We had to put the basic skills on hold while I helped him navigate the search for a new place to live. He joined a group of students living in a house in the University District. Despite second thoughts and requests to return home, Ousman was done with and grateful for that phase of his life.

Next in his sequence of life's milestones and cultural adaptation was the divorce papers. My professionalism was tested in how much I helped and advocated for him in what was a high stakes game with winners and losers and collisions of dreams, cultures, and possessions. His wife was twelve years his senior at sixty-two.

"I know a little about divorce," I said sheepishly. "After all, I've had two so far." I offered a perspective of the pitfalls and pratfalls he might encounter.

His Gambian family was more tribal in its makeup and orientation. He spoke of a book that was passed down by generation after generation. It was now kept with his sister—it is the history of his extended family and the bonds that bind. His trademark comment is a warm, heartfelt "Thank you *so* much!" There is an expanded definition of brother and sister and family leadership.

Their divorce proceeded with a health insurance glitch or two. The wife number one was needed to provide continuity for the eyes of the US immigration departments in a story that soon follows.

After the separation, I could see his depressed state, did a check on his life in general as opener one day and asked if he was meeting any new friends, women in particular. He was familiar with Craigslist with his many purchases, finding a home, auto parts, jobs.

I asked him in a professional tone, "Have you ever looked at the Craigslist personals?"

"Uh, whu—?" he would respond to me. "What are you talking about?"

Knowing what possible posts could be, I backtracked when I remembered the school internet policies could be compromised. I told him if he wanted more help with this, he should visit me at my home. He took me up on the offer a couple of times in the following months, and I helped him respond to a dating website.

I got us connected with the Democratic party. We spent a day as volunteers by doorbelling to remind Fremont's voters to remember to mail in their ballots for the 2012 presidential election. I would introduce Ousman at resident's doors as "one of our newest US citizens." He was ebullient. Ousman embodies the immigrant effect in which he takes the rights and responsibilities of US citizenship very dutifully along with the pride. His Muslim beliefs were never imposed, not once. We talk every election. He asks my advice on ballot measures.

But once again, life and cultures would collide.

Ousman discovered he had a daughter at home in the Gambia, eighteen, Sallie is her name.

Ramatoulaye (Ramou), her mother, was Ousman's girlfriend when they were in their early years. Her father disapproved of the relationship with Ousman and disliked his extended family. Father moved Ramou away to another village to marry a man of his liking.

Only after the father died could Ramou reveal the truth of Ousman's paternity to him and to Sallie.

Sallie searched for and found Ousman through his sister, Haddy. Sallie made clear she wanted to go and be with her father. Haddy helped manage her immigration to Seattle. It was an arduous process at best with Immigration asking for a photo proof of his relationship with his daughter chronicled over their separate lives.

The question of paternity was answered with DNA test results through the US Consulate.

Ramou said Ousman could "have" his daughter if he paid her $2,500 US. Eventually, the arrangement got worked out. Father and daughter got acquainted with exchanged phone calls, e-mails, and Skype video conferencing.

At the same time, this story was breaking. We mutually agreed it was time to end our regularly scheduled sessions. Maybe it was when I said, while pressing him to schedule taking the CDL exam, I blurted out matter-of-factly, "After two years, it could be easily three more years of study, and if we don't get that test taken, there'll be two

old men sitting here instead of just one." His work hours were changing, and he was able to get overtime from a second maintenance
company. It was a way to get twelve hours a day out of him without
paying an overtime rate.

It was a good thing I got tickets to the annual fundraising
breakfast for Literacy Source that spring morning at Seattle Pacific
University in 2012. Ousman was the student speaker. He has a stage
presence that appears regal. There wasn't a dry eye in the house, least
of all mine when he completed his eloquent talk sharing his journey
with donors, staff, family, and students.

Ousman speaking at Literacy Source annual luncheon.

I assisted Ousman as far as I could in his "instant daughter's"
immigration to Seattle. He went prepared with the right paperwork
for his immigration lawyer. The process took well over a year before
twenty-one-year-old Sallie called Seattle home. I got to meet her in
my home when I helped her prepare a résumé for employment. She
looked like she was unsure of what to think of me. Her paperwork
was surprisingly complete, along with her command of English. In
the interim, Ousman married again to a beautiful young woman

from Senegal, who was then living in the New York City area.[†] They were married back home with her family hosting the ceremony. I helped him with some travel documents and legal papers.

He was able to purchase a home in Everett with his new spouse and daughter joining him as coworkers in the janitorial service. He navigated the process impressively.

I wonder about how he's doing but know he's never very far. Last year, he called to say hello. His concern was a traffic accident, small, but it was his fault. I reassured him his insurance company would take care of all of it, and his rate might increase.

In his youthful middle age, Ousman developed glaucoma, which impacted becoming a CDL license holder and driver. "But hey," I pointed outside at the Seattle gridlock and said, "you still wanna drive in *that?*" He still has visions of the open road to see this beautiful continent.

On another occasion, he stopped by, and we prepared a written request to his employer and union for a six-week leave of absence to return home to the Gambia and help the patriarch of his family put his affairs in order. We priced round trip flights from Seattle to Dakar and solar panels to carry to his family there.

Just recently, while I was busy making arrangements after my mother passed away, he called to offer his condolences and ask for help with paperwork related to medical bills. Life and grieving were put into perspective with more clarity when he told me his young wife had died suddenly, unexpectedly, from medical complications in a local hospital.[†] He accepted the fate with a resilience I could only admire.

Ousman called me once on Father's Day to say hello and speak of his dream life here and express his gratitude to me for helping him through this journey. "I would be nothing without you as my teacher. Thank you *so* much, Bill."

"No, no," I say humbly, "I'm the lucky one here." My follow up question, "Then maybe things will slow down enough and you can

---

[†] Ousman's second wife died recently from cancer.

take that CDL written test soon?" I'd ask it then and would ask it today if we talked.

"Yes, yes, Bill," he replies. We laugh tentatively with each other.

The best way to find yourself is to lose
yourself in the service of others.

—Mahatma Gandhi

Making that move has made all the difference.

Sheree's a Friend to Most, Except Maybe Herself

Sheree says it would be Zsa Zsa or Eva Gabor, the Hungarian accented sisters who were made famous by their glamour and, of course, their Hungarian accents. "Dahling"—she says that's the most natural representation of herself if there were a movie made of her life. She keeps her hair tastefully but butcherly short, all one length. Her eyes are deep, and her makeup is always perfect. Her frame has taken on more weight lately, which limits her energy and ability to navigate the city's streets with places to go and things to do.

She now resides in Lower Queen Anne but for two decades lived, loved, and learned in Fremont raising her son, Lionel, now a teacher with two kids of his own.

Sheree was born Jewish in the Czech Republic while it was called Czechoslovakia. She's nearing the Medicare era of her life. Her parents in earnest were the first settlers in newly formed Israel. Her earliest memory is Israel being nothing but rocks.

Israeli national citizenship required her military service as a young woman in the Air Force. Sheree fell in love with a dashing young pilot. Love led her to follow him to medical school and residency in New York City to become an anesthesiologist. While helping him through her support, she found herself pregnant yet unmarried.

The dashing pilot would deny paternity and switch the blood sample in the process of disproving his paternity. But she says she has always loved him.

As a single mother, she moved to Chicago, then West Hollywood, and then to the early days of Fremont, as it developed into the center of the universe.

Upon meeting for the first time, Gladys (my mother) and Sheree asked each other why the other never married after losing the love of their lives in the 1990s.

"You never remarried?" Gladys asked.

"I never thought I would find a love as good as that one," replied Sheree rather matter-of-factly.

"Ohhh, aww, me too!" was Gladys's response as their eyes welled up, their hearts visibly melted, at the same time there was a bond creating legend.

I first met Sheree on the street as she passed me in front of my new town house without missing a beat to her rhythm of walking her little aging yapper dog, Kellie, sightseeing, pushed in a child's stroller.

"How many people live in that place?"

'Two of us," I say.

"Tearing down houses to build four more is the reason our rent is going up, making it hard to stay here."

I invited her in for a drink to meet my then-partner, followed by dinner where a fast friendship ensued.

Her comments prompted me to organize our neighbors to host a block party after Fremont's Solstice Parade with the band that would characterize us that covered the oldies.

Kellie could cross his front paws and look like he was praying. It was something the dog must have prayed for, to ride in the comfort of the stroller, not having to climb the hill from Thirty-Sixth Avenue to Thirty-Ninth Avenue. Sheree was a walking contradiction for motherhood and dog walking.

Yet Kellie lived until he was twenty-two, that was after a heart and liver transplants were performed right here in Fremont by a partnership of naturopathic physicians and their sponsors.

Aunt Jude and Sheree had no love lost between each other. One of them grew angry at the other because of misplaced jealous intentions of one of Fremont's most eligible, Benny. Fur flew when they crossed paths at our first party, during and after the annual solstice parade famous for the painted naked bicyclists. I let that one go until the identity of the mystery man that created the rift was revealed.

I just won't put nor ask both in the same room.

Sheree also developed a mistrust for my ex-partner, the Colonel. She could see through his drunken antics. She claimed he grabbed her with an attempted smart-ass push that could have resulted in a fall down the town house stairs. The Colonel might have been capable of it. The abuser does their thing when there are no witnesses, you know. One of them was jealous of the other, putting me in the middle to distract their judgments, attentions, and intentions. I was flattered she was right up front with me in her desires for romance, no matter the persuasion of past or present conquests.

Before she came here, in West Hollywood, Sheree and her one child, Lionel, rented a cottage from a wealthy gay couple. The men really helped out this single mom with occasional child care for Lionel and late rent payments. They both got a California-style life ripe with celebrity culture. The landlords did more than be helpful to Lionel when it came to thievery of his innocence, as in molested. Sheree learned this as wedding plans were in progress. That is the first story I heard.

Later, she would tell she knew nothing of her son's molestation.

Overtime, she changed her story. The second story was that she needed to flee California and had moved twenty-five years ago to Fremont so that Lionel could have a better education.

Being a single mom was hard, and all her attention was spent on Lionel through his youth. Sheree's love life seemed nonexistent, except for discreet encounters, peccadillos, that were hastily executed, sometimes regretted. She was celibate and too pooped to party is her annotated description of those formative years.

Lionel would marry a University of Washington Medical Center intern that he met through JewMatch.com. The bride's family, flush with money, planned a lavish wedding for two hundred at a golf country club in California. Sheree was beside herself deciding what to wear and feeling inadequate that the only invitees from the groom's side of the family were Sheree, her brother and sister-in-law from Tel Aviv, and the groom, of course. I helped her find airfare to take her brother and sister-in-law to San Francisco and Los Angeles after the wedding.

The plan was for the three of them to rent a car in Seattle after their arrival and sightsee a drive south for the wedding.

Five days before the wedding, it was after only the first one-night reunion, there was an epic argument among the three, and the siblings left in a huff to return to their adopted mother country, leaving Sheree holding the bag and airline tickets. The mother of the groom was now solo, the guilt for the symbolism all around her that was in her control and out of her control. Laments were voiced repeatedly, speculating her son would move to California to find work with his bride and leave her all alone here in Seattle to have no one to kvetch over. Like an Israeli pit bull, Sheree would focus on the liabilities that lay ahead rather than the assets that could be derived in the next chapter of life after motherhood on the grand scale of a kosher mom.

Sheree's health would plague her in this new era, booze, pain pills, weed, cigarettes, and pastries would fill her days. She had Lasik surgery for her cataracts. It might have given her perfect vision today, except she twitched when one lens was being cut.

We lost touch with my move down the street on Francis Avenue. I bumped into her just a couple of times, and I got a call from her a while back telling me she had spent a week in the hospital.

While standing for the Metro bus downtown, a crazy woman came at her and hit her about the head and torso with a baseball bat given to the perpetrator at the Bat Giveaway night the Seattle Mariners baseball team has every year at T-Mobile Park. Her attacker was never charged for the assault. This time, it was thievery of hope she experienced.

We got together last week when we agreed to meet at the Fremont Sunday Market. It was her chance to visit old friends and catch up on the gossip and changes to the neighborhood. She needed sympathy, but she also needed possibilities and a kick in the butt. I reminded her of the lesson she taught me as a market vendor, how to attract customers to my merchandise. We hold it in our hand, we appear to negotiate price complete with hand gestures and voila, a crowd starts to form.

I encouraged Sheree by giving her my story and my pathway out of the doldrums. It was through community service that I developed the momentum to break my depressive state cocoon. I shared my experiences as a sixty-five-year-old and told her to find wonder in the world, think *we,* not *me* so much, pay karma forward and look online.

"*Now* stop right there," I tell her. "*You don't* have a computer? You don't know how to navigate the internet?

You don't have an e-mail address? "Well, that phone you're holding is a computer. You can go online, send e-mail, text messages. *And* you can walk around with it in your hand like everyone else."

I ask her for her phone number. I enter it into my phone and send Sheree a text message with the expectation she answers and respond back to me with a text. She is humored, but I don't think convinced. The text message was never returned to me.

I told her, "One thing I've learned in my sixth decade on the planet. Learn something new *every* day along with the act of expressing yourself creatively, artistically."

Maybe Sheree's stuck in the habit of putting up fences instead of opening gates. I ask her after we eat if she feels like Zsa Zsa or Eva Gabor playing her in the movie.

"They are both dead," she said. "You know, I prefer the name Natalie after Natalie Wood. You know, she was murdered on that boat. Otherwise, if she went overboard, she would have lived anyway because wood floats."

"*Huh?*"

At the time, I failed to get the humor she was trying to present. She then would clarify to me the line, and I ruined her joke. The movie star question by me was my way of making her lighten up and know that I know she has a story to tell.

I take her out to a late lunch at the new Irish Bar here, O'Donnell's, featuring real Irishmen as bartenders. We have a draft beer that for once doesn't have that bitter hop taste. Sheree asks and keeps the attention of the non-Irish-accented waiter who reveals he's married to a Jewish woman once he hears Sheree's Czech accent.

She wants me to go online when we walk back to my place and find her an inexpensive cruise. I find one for fifteen days on Norwegian Cruise Line, going from Miami to Seattle for $799 inside per person double occupancy. She's ready to jump on it but didn't realize there'd be $450 more in government fees and taxes. As a single, she would also need to double the per-person-double-occupancy inside cabin price for a single occupancy.

She won't have any of that.

I explain, I explain, I try to conceal the initial prices on other cruises giving her the total at the end. She wants to pay $799. After twenty minutes of the kibbitz, I think my head will explode from my ears, mouth, and eye sockets. I drive her back over the hill to her Lower Queen Anne residence. We promise each other we will be in touch, we say our goodbyes, I give her a hug, and she gives me a kiss.

A year later, we bump into each other at the Fremont Sunday Market. She's gaunt and has a roller stroller attached to one foot and leg. It is a warm friendship she and I have. It is a rich friendship that gets deep quickly. And it is a friendship best played out with chance meetings she and I have.

Two Stores, Two Managers, One Family, One Customer

It's the stuff that fills the day. We all have that one or more convenience stores we transact with regularly; usually, it's close to home, within walking distance, dog walkable distance, if we have one; and for those times, we need to explode from the inside out for a change of scene, walking away from a scene or to interact with humans at the most convenient level to attend to our needs, thirsts, and hungers. In Fremont, it's the Fremart. And the 7-Eleven with gas pumps is only steps away.

Evolution of Fremont Hotel to M&S Deli to the Fremart.

Each offers the same fare. The 7-Eleven's product assortments are certainly more data-driven. Their marketing strategy to double dose that candy bar by keeping the price low, I'm sure, ups their bottom line. I buy beer, chips, candy, ice cream, phone cards, apple fritters, nonalcoholic drinks, and occasionally, rarely, a corn-doggette or burrito-needs-a-home. Oh yes, heartburn bandages like Pepto, GERD pills, and chalk in a bottle or roll are forethought or afterthought to my visits. Lotto is blotto.

The Fremart, formerly known as M&S Deli, is a little more personality-driven or homegrown. For thirty-six years, Moses ran the deli and rented the space from building owners of the old Fremont Hotel. The building still has tenants upstairs who share one bathroom down the hall. The corner parking strip is filled with Juan, the Guerilla Gardener's, handiwork. The Fremont Hotel Building is either a teardown with its buckled front above its unlikely corner door, which would have been a load-bearing corner. It could have been a preservationist's dream with the turn of the nineteenth-century craftsman woodwork and glass atrium rooftop.

Now from across the counter, a bespectacled, attractive young woman seems an unlikely store owner and heir apparent to the reins of the Fremart. She'll usually greet you with a cheerful eye-contacted, "Hey-ey," and end each sale with "Have a good one," only more droll. Parmvier runs the Fremart twelve hours a day or more and seven to eight days a week. At the tender age of twenty-six, a graduate of Ballard High School, she went to North Seattle College, and got her degree in pharmacy tech. She tried that pill tech, hated it, and her father, John, made her the offer to join him in the family business.

The family also owns and operates the 7-Eleven. The challenge to us, their target clientele, is that they have a monopoly for our discretionary dollars. Their extended family of aunts, cousins, and uncles all live nearby with John being the first in the clan to immigrate from India to Germany to the center of the universe.

Moses's departure, albeit abrupt, was inevitable after all those years. He was well into retirement demographics, tired after opening the Fremart every day, every week, every month, and year. Parmvier is a youthful and hopeful presence in the neighborhood, protected by her dad and her family.

It is what it is. This is where I come in. Goddamn it, I wish I could keep my mouth shut when it comes to teachable moments in retail, but you can't take the store away from an old DECA teacher. It was thirty-three years of teaching marketing that strangles me to say it when somebody needs to hear it, especially if I'm a customer. Granted, I'm a lot less strident and arrogant in my delivery, but with this short time left, I'm going to make it memorable, or I walk away. Suffer the fool who gets back in my face, who ups the attitude at which I think is a helpful observation and suggestion. As a customer, we have a whole lot more license for attitude, especially if it will benefit future transactions.

Early after the family took over the Fremart operation, I began to notice and became mildly annoyed at the amount of garbage left on the sidewalk and in the street and back area of the Fremart. It was well after that grace for newbie status had lapsed. I said to Parmvier one evening, "You know, while you're not busy, you should get out and pick up a few pieces of the garbage out there." She insisted she was too busy, and that considering their customers, they didn't care about how it looks. I think she was referring to the drunks.

I gave her my best heartfelt but pissed off "But this is our home, where we live." It was an emotionally charged moment. "Would you go to a restaurant that had garbage all over the street in front and want its food?"

Shortly after, arrangements were made for a street person to attend to the sidewalk.

I would frequently pick up garbage and return it to their store's recycle inside the store to quietly make a point.

Now, Juan, our guerilla gardener and star resident of the Fremont Hotel, has the corner as his canvass. Case 1.0 solved for now.

Just a few more steps up Thirty-Sixth is the 7-Eleven, right next to the new multiuse apartment building with Sartori's marijuana store on its first floor.

It was late one night. I wanted to buy a can of beer and pack of cigarettes before the 11:00 p.m. news. Dizzy rode his bike alongside.

I bought two cans of Mikes Harder, advertised for two for $4, and a pack of cigarettes. As he rang up my purchases, I noted the readout to my left read "Lottery Tickets." I was handed a handful of coins, no mention of the sale total was made.

I then questioned, "Hey, those Mike's were two for $4 right over here the sign says, 'two for $4.'"

Indignant, the related family cashier marched me over to the fridge and said declaratively, "That's a mistake. Someone moved the 'two for $4' sign."

"Wait a minute now, I've been buying those for the past month." I countered his claim.

"Oh, those are old signs," my cashier dismisses me. He then blames me for moving the sign.

I see a younger male relative stocking merchandise. I implore this one to help me make sense of the prices. "Oh, we have no control nor access to the pricing system, that's 7-Eleven's."

By then, I was mad and put it to the relative. "I want you to ring it up like I bought it. It said 'Lottery Ticket' on the screen."

It's illegal for retailers to purchase their own lottery tickets, and this one was stealing it from his family owner.

Soon, number two brother, Ron, comes out to leave. I see him and start to state my case. He motions to the cashier and says, "Give him what he wants."

I interject, "Hey, why don't your people state the amount of sale or change amount counted back?"

"Nobody wants to hear that," he says.

The cashier gives me another clump of change and motions with both hands as if to shoo me away, "You *go!*"

It was a time of reckoning, "*Now* I want you to ring it all up like it was supposed to be, and we can complete the sale. And I can get my correct change from the $20 bill."

I was incensed, to say the least, went home, and typed up a statement describing point by point of my experience. I handed it to John the next morning.

"We'll look into it, and I'll get back to you."

John didn't get back. I had to ask a couple more times. Once, I caught both him and the relative together in the store while pumping my gas.

I asked, "Well, now that I have you both in the same room, what about that sale with the Mike's?'

"Oh no, it wasn't him," John says, "another relative."

I later ask Parmvier if she's heard of my tangle with the 7-Eleven. I was looking for some recognition or apology. It was if I kept trying to hang on to a former self, and my behavior couldn't let go. I was told I was a "valued customer and neighbor" with the warmest of expression. It was all I needed, and it's been mutual neighborly interactions ever since.

There is responsibility being a retailer and responsibility being a customer. Now my change is usually counted out. I smile and wave when we pass, always ready to engage with the merchants of Fremont. I pick up the garbage on the street as a sign of respect for Fremont and their business and clientele, including the need to keep our dignity, admitting we were right. After all, we are thrown together as denizens in this place.

Youth and hopefulness defined, Parmvier presides at this corner of the center of the universe, that I think has everything life needs. I visit and pay my respects with dollars at one or two of their businesses every day. As a customer, whatever that means anymore, it gives me a say in whatever strikes my fancy, sometimes it's valid; usually, it is. I pick my fights, look for those teachable moments, and play my music.

Parmvier is first-generation East Indian. As the middle child, more likely to have friends outside the nuclear family, she wants to get her degree in business and get into the field of property management. She is poised on the dilemma of whether to leave Seattle or stay in the safe cocoon of her entrepreneurial family. With a foot in each culture, her decision will make all the difference in the capacity of her potential, whatever that means anymore. I know she'll do the right thing with her dad and her family's blessings.

Hopes and Dreams Pinned to the Perimeter of Our Habits

June 2012, November 2016, and June 2019

Mary Anne Dickerson and Ed Hirschler are the principals in See Monster Window Cleaning Service and in each other's lives. There's a good chance Fremonsters have seen them daily, know them, or may be doing business with them. The name of their business, See Monster, is a metaphor; earth's species adapted from living in the sea to dominate the land.

Business Adaptation

Always previously on foot, the duo, Mary Anne, with her big backpack and Ed with his hand truck carrying the tools of their trade, exhibit a resilience that is immediately evident. It's easy to get to know and trust them, and both prefer being known by, and knowing people, on a first-name basis.

This month, they purchased an excellent condition 1998 Ford Windstar van with a loan from Mary Anne's dad. Their sole intent: to take See Monster to the next level. They want to expand their reach and transport more tools to ply their trade.

Mary Anne's business degree from Central Washington University, and some hard-earned life skills, provide the marketing, accounting, clerical skills, heart, and determination that provide the structure of their ten-year partnership in life and with See Monster.

Ed, with his charismatic smile and ready-to-help attitude, provides the sweat and labor. They form an inseparable pair, like a two-piece puzzle, joined at the hip, completing each other's sentences, and sometimes both talking at once. Together ten years, they have, at times, lived in their vehicle.

Personal Adaptation

Mary Anne grew up in Port Townsend, adopted. At the age of nine, she had bone and brain cancer and endured over three years of radiation and chemotherapy. The trauma has left her with gaps in memory from that time. Hers was a development that, she admits with a patient, catlike presence, alternately made her lose her innocence early yet stunted her in the path to maturity.

Today, in her early forties, she does her best to live "la Pura Vida" in Fremont fashion and still manage her hopes and health fears that occasionally manifest in long-term depression.

Ed, born in Oklahoma, a Southern boy, was uprooted to California as a child. He was lured to Seattle in the 1990s by the grunge music movement and his dreams of being a drummer in a band. He had many gigs and even auditioned for Alice in Chains. Gonzo journalist Hunter S. Thompson is his hero, and he shares that icon's love of music, life, words, and writing.

Ed admits his boundless personality needs Mary Anne to give him boundaries, confidence, and direction. Together, they help each other keep their demons in check.

See Monster Plans a Future in Fremont

See Monster's regular clients, as described by Ed in cheerleader fashion, include Condor Electronics, Speed Queen Laundromat, M&S Deli, Caravan Carpets, and Pacific Inn Pub. They also provide day labor to various people and businesses around the area. The day after Deluxe Junk closed their doors, Ed and Mary Anne were recruited to help move the bones and remains of thirty-four years in business.

The pair are full of hopes and dreams for See Monster. Ed cites his goals as "become contributing members of society" and "grow a business to a successful level." They've started developing marketing tools, such as business cards, logo art, and once they can afford them, a website, uniforms, and hats. Ed is grateful when he describes the technical assistance and "training" he's received from Puget Sound Reprographics.

They love Fremont and plan to stay. They hope to move from their cramped studio apartment, with their cats, to a larger place. They are saddened by some of the recent business closures, especially the Buckaroo Tavern, yet people are "friendly and easy to approach here," Ed says. The Wednesday community dinner at the Doric Lodge is a regular outing, and the Ballard Food Bank is "one of the best."

Ed and Mary Anne, never the types to wallow, sit, or be couch potatoes, enthusiastically participate in local community festivals and street scenes. The Fremont Fair photo collection on Facebook includes Ed in his signature gorilla suit with Mary Anne next to him in black, looking catlike.

Mary Anne as cat and Ed as a gorilla.

Last weekend, Ed got out the suit—cleaned and combed—for the Fair while Mary Anne continued living one of her nine lives at his side. To hire See Monster, give her a call.

Mary Anne Dickerson and Ed Hirschler of See Monster—Fremont residents building a Fremont business. Photo by Bill Crossman, May 2012.

Ed Hirschler of See Monster shows off the tools of his trade and the company's new mode of transportation. Photo by Bill Crossman, May 2012.

The Fremont couple, Ed Hirschler and Mary Anne Dickerson, partners in business and in life. Photo by Bill Crossman, May 2012.

The gorilla at the Fremont Fair, June 2011,
the alternate personality of Ed Hirschler.
Photo provided by See Monster.

In 2016

Shortly after this story appeared in the *Fremocentrist* in 2012, Ed and Mary Anne got a little drunk and high at their apartment in Fremont at the top of the universe, near Woodland Park Zoo. They live in a hoarder's haven with their three cats, all of whom are considered their children. Mary Anne fell asleep that night, and Ed, in a lapse of judgment, drove the car down the hill to hang out in their new rig and impress his Fremonster friends and acquaintances at the Nectar Lounge and club scene.

Somehow, Ed encountered Ronnie, a crazed interloper, with that danger look in his eyes. Ronnie and Ed got into a fight, fists flung far into their space, and Ed lost several teeth from his winning smile. Seattle police officers were called. Ed, with no driver's license, was arrested and jailed. Mary Anne was beside herself, and of course, she said little but showed signs of disappointment in Ed. He served probation for the next eight months and could not drink alcohol. The van was damaged in the melee, and to make matters worse, two months later, its transmission went out.

I grew to be wary of any food or baked goods they would bring me after setting foot in their place. Their apartment sits next to four large new town houses, where there previously sat an old craftsman home that was so infested with bedbugs. They had to demolish it and take all the yard dirt away.

We continued to socialize whenever they would drop by my place. Ed with his grape soda in a bottle and mixed with whiskey or vodka or tequila.

Our visits usually coincided with the last days of the month when they wanted to sell me something so that Ed could get his alcohol. They both gained a lot of weight, and Ed qualified for disability alongside Mary Anne. I could see signs of depression in both.

Mary Anne's mother felt they should marry and offered to pay for their wedding. It was a small affair that took place at the top of the Space Needle with a wedding dinner following. I wanted to attend the event, but no invitations were offered, except for an offer to join the wedding party for $120.

They devised a wild plan for a honeymoon. They would rent a van to drive to Disneyland with their three cats. No one was trusted to care for their feline babies.

The honeymoon road trip was aborted near Redding, California, when the cats got sick, and their plan to keep them in the vehicle went sour with the summer heat. They drove back to Fremont with their cats.

Ed was able to get a set of dentures that improved his self-esteem, but its lasting effects reverted him back to a 1980s rocker mentality. Mary Anne would try to keep it together. She tried to lose weight, but in the end, they were both incapable of changing the habits that limited them both in the first place. Most of their clients went out of business, and their friends grew weary of their antics, which wore thin on their friendships and pocketbooks.

I asked them not to continually stop by without notification. Ed would stand out on the street; I could look out the eighteen windows and see him, phone to his ear, as my phone rang. He would ask to come inside my place. I grew weary and testy and refused to assist with their schemes for booze money from me. He would call and say he had a gift for me. I helped them be vendors at the Fremont Sunday Market. They were both developing their own styles of artistic expression—Ed with his folk-art Space Needle pieces and Mary Anne with her geometric drawings in colored pens and pencils.

I just don't see them much anymore.

In 2019

Out of the blue, a few months back, I received a call from Mary Anne. She and Ed split up.

I'm not sure which of them and their demons were the catalysts for the break. But this was a pair who completed each other's sentences.

The landlord wanted to reclaim their hoarder's haven apartment. Health standards demanded it. It also served as a wedge in their Jack and Jill relationship. "Jack and Jill went up the hill / to fetch a pail of water. Jack fell down and broke his crown / and Jill came tumbling after."

Mary Anne called me to say hello and with the news and a status report. She was living in Port Townsend at her mother's. She had plans. Mary Anne lost weight and was ready for more of life's lessons. The divorce proceedings were in motion.

A few months ago, there were reports of only seeing Ed solo on foot in Fremont. A fight occurred, and the rumor was the principals were carted off to jail. The question was heard on the street, "Wasn't that Ed in that fight?"

I just don't see them much anymore.

Bob the Quiver of Fremont

I first met Bob the Quiver right after moving to my current address. That's right, after leaving my first Fremont address and the second long-term relationship in my adult life.

Aunt Jude had inherited all that money from her brother's estate. Her work was done here, which opened this home in our funky fourplex. Bob shared his experience in messy divorces, helping me to face the music instead of disappearing somewhere in Mexico.

We faced the music in other ways with our love and appreciation of legendary musicians of the 1970s like Leon Russell, Little Feat, Lowell George, Joni Mitchell, and Randy Newman. We attended our first gathering of gray hairs when we saw Leon play a few blocks away one fine summer evening at the Tractor Tavern in Ballard. Whenever he stops by, I will put on some new or old music as a soundtrack for our time together.

I am putting my garden to bed this beautiful summer evening in the dog days of August. It's that time of night to transition from the recorded music to something on television. The gate of the white picket fence is open, and up rides Bob, tanned, toned, fine-tuned, and tired. He chirps in his chipper voiced, "Hi, I was in the neighborhood, and I saw you were home, thought I'd stop by." He looks distinguished with the new closely cropped salt-and-pepper-shaded beard. You can still pick up a twinge of his Boston accent in his speech.

I'm always glad to see Bob, but it's getting to be a regular daily occurrence—the arrival of a friend, acquaintance, and even a one-night stand at my doorstep, unannounced, that I greet warmly or turn away from my door. These accidental visitors, tourists to my life, caused my neighbor to question if I was selling drugs. I laughed when I first heard these false suspicions. And maybe to a casual observer, I would describe it more like the premise of a kids' TV show, like *J. P. Patches*, *Pee-wee's Playhouse*, or even *Sesame Street* with drop-in characters to boost the entertainment value of the plot.

I tell myself when assessing the quality of life here in the center of the universe to deal with it, enjoy it, appreciate it, and celebrate it or *move*. I've been told I collect strays. Pardon my subconscious digression here.

It's great to see Bob, survivor of lymphoma cancer, riding his bike again. He beat a disease that rendered him paralyzed and on crutches just a short time ago. For time spent overcoming this hurdle in his life, Bob had many epiphanies as a result of which I was lucky to be included now as a valued friend rather than just an upgraded casual acquaintance. Bob's cancer allowed his heart to get bigger and his arms to grow longer.

A trained, certified urban planner by trade, Bob today lives, for the most part, off the grid. Except for the charities he accesses with his health issues and HIV status, he pretty much leaves a small footprint or paper trail for his own moral reasons, coupled with the entanglements of two messy divorces with a daughter from each.

He possesses an informed sensibility of the brave new world that's ahead for all of us, coupled with a reckless abandonment many would envy. He'll make and take "life hacks" to a higher level than most. He's my go-to guy for these best practical solutions to saving fingertips and sanity.

A few years back, after meeting each other, Bob would stop by here, stay a day or so, and do my dishes for me in my kitchen with the ghostly presence. This was during the learning-to-act-like-a-child phase of my retirement. We would laugh and cheerfully, share war stories, and solve the problems of the world over a smoke and a beverage. He has the skill to create a feast out of thin air while I just opened cans.

Bob the Quiver has many adventure stories from crisscrossing the continent solely by using a rideshare posting on the Craigslist website. For little or no cost, trading work or a few pennies for gas, he sees the world and meets fascinating people, including a parcel of crazies.

But those messy divorces have made co-parenting difficult. He's emotionally vested as a dad, but the net financials of his subsistence-only lifestyle and positive HIV status make difficult the authentic transparency needed by a man, a cancer survivor, nearing sixty-two years. He's been through two hip replacement surgeries. Bob's knees and mind are next.

Bob's a bisexual man. He has a lady friend who is fascinated by his carefree life. She lives vicariously through his adventures and only asks for companionship in return. She's financially comfortable and gladly covers the costs of having a colorful companion in their cultural interests of arts and leisure. And that was then. But this is now.

His lady friend in the last year has retired from her career, and he's joined her in hosting a wedding for her daughter and welcoming to the world a grandchild. The luggage got heavier, and the wings got clipped. They have purchased a nice piece of acreage overlooking Hood Canal with the intent to design, build, and inhabit a series of living possibilities, sustainable, and monumental in legacy and legend.

The lady friend is now a significant-other relationship with conditions in a world of compartments and commitments. I tell him,

"The third time's the charm, Bob." It's back to the future with more middle-class values to uphold, defend, and upend.

It has been a journey witnessing Bob's coats of many colors and trading his loose feet for more luggage of the emotional kind that matches his landscape. Bob's a practicing Quaker and regularly attends their open-forum prayer meetings. His character is framed by his Masonic youth DeMolay training.

Attending a candidates' forum for city council with Bob recently, I was impressed with his engagement with participants. I do believe he has a future in these public arenas.

If all works out well, this summer, he'll achieve a trifecta on a trip to Kansas City: (1) completing a lifelong bucket list item to see a home baseball game in every major league baseball stadium in the country; (2) to attend a fifty-year reunion of the DeMolay; and (3) to reunite with a daughter still estranged from his messier divorce.

Life has gotten more complicated, and he's willing to accept it. He seems to take it in stride although his need to vent frustrations has taken on a higher pitch. What I admire is, the degree of experience, the amount of wonder he still holds for the world, and the hopes he has for humanity and the planet.

This night, while I put my dinner in the oven, put my new Little Feat Basement tapes CD on, we share a drink and a smoke, and without him taking the time for a breath in between sentences, much less me getting to get a word in, he tells me all about their recent road trip across Canada and back through the Midwest. We laugh, we tear up, we tell stories, discuss the music, search the truth out, and most of all, trust each other. He's tired this night after spending the last twenty-four hours chasing rainbows. He asks if he can borrow my electric clippers. Instead, I give him the battery clippers. It could be the last time I see them. He leaves me some fruit he got at the food bank. I give him a hug and an unexpected kiss as he left for home a few blocks away on his bicycle.

I won't ever complain about drop-in visitors again.

Two Crossmen

In the bipolar, venture out on the extremes world, light and dark, hot and cold, oldest and youngest worlds of Aunt Jude and I, we take similar paths to thrive or shrivel in retreat. You may recall the story about Jude and me bumping into each other at the Fremart after a fifty-two-year gap in time. She had gone crazy, and as she says, "to a dark place" after a distinguished career channeling her charges as a "midwife to death" or hospice nurse.

You could say I had challenges as well. I had ditched a twenty-eight-year marriage to assume my gay identity at the peak of my education career at age forty-six.

Jude, just three years older than I, at seventy-one had come of age in the ages of opposition, confrontation, conflagration, manipulation, postindustrial carbon-based gadgets, princess phones, and full of shit memories. My dad, who was Jude's oldest brother, disguised his real cheapskate ways, inevitably to arise, preferring public school cost-free without those financial obligations associated with parents who care. But we are both old enough to have had decent educations as children. Jude had a proper Catholic education, therefore beautiful handwriting, along with access to the most off-color jokes. Me, as I've said many a time, I am so full of bullshit. I stink.

We've been postwar (which war?). We grew up when dreams could be found on television. Since then, this country lost journalistic integrity, and with it, our trust in today's institutions. There's red and blue talk radio, suburban, with white men, white bread, white privilege that was before cell phones; and changes spurred on by a digitally connected, demystifying-democratized world, that is busted and hell-bent to live in a place taking selfies as a path to fame and maybe reaching perfection in life as a reality TV show star in this new internet-aged renaissance, the likes that humanity can't grasp the extremes, the heights and the lows, winners and losers, we love to hate and hate to love.

Pick up the damn cell phone when needed but give priority to those in the same room as you. Please!

Aunt Jude, a.k.a. Judy Crossman, was written off by her five older siblings, of which my dad was the oldest and lead sociopath in a clan of individuals instinctively selfish. They prided themselves on upper lower-class values and nonconformity were distinctive in how they made their marks in the world with little sense of consequences.

With her sunbonnet, perfectly coifed shoulder-length blond-gray formerly red hair, flip-flops, straight-line suit skirts, she's child-like in wonder. And, it should be mentioned, Jude is a titan of late-night talk radio. She is a frequent caller articulate and respected by progressive blue listeners and hosts.

Ten years ago or so, it was Jude and Superbeans Bob. (He also was website manager for J. P. Patches before J. P.'s death, that's another story.) As local regular callers to the Mike Malloy National Radio Show, with Mike's blessing, they raised in a short period almost $30,000 to send *every* prosecuting attorney in every state and every county in these United States a copy of a book. I'm sure you never heard of that book *The Prosecution of George W. Bush for Murder* sent along with a personal letter signed by its author, former Los Angeles prosecutor for the Charles Manson family murderers and Pulitzer Prize winner for his book about it, *Helter Skelter*, the dapper, Vincent Bugliosi.

Considering the distinct possibility Bugliosi had *no* chance for mainstream promotion and distribution, he supported the effort with his own money and time. I met Vince and Bob Superbeans at a meeting that Jude asked to attend. She recruited me as her driver one night to the Seattle W Hotel. The conference room was filled with mostly idealistic progressives, holdouts from the Vietnam era protests, and a dark energy of suited undercover government agents, and the remainder who wanted to volunteer. Never heard of that book, huh?

In Bugliosi's hardcover book, he lays out the case for prosecuting GW Bush for war crimes in the events leading up to the demise of Iraq and Saddam Hussein's overthrow. Today, GW and Darth Vader wannabe, Dick Cheney, vice president, reportedly cannot leave the states for fear; people like the Germans will arrest them for war crimes and prosecute for murder. I helped Jude and Superbeans prepare the mailing of the books paid for by volunteer donors like you. In the end, life went on, books were sold, word spread, and a couple of DAs from liberal northeast states, close to the end of their careers, expressed interest. I was proud of what my aunt Jude accomplished.

It's true that line about how *one* person can change the world.

The cynical me for a brief period was overshadowed by that old friend, my idealist me. Vince died, Jude invested her million-dollar inheritance in her family and peace initiatives. Superbeans Bob moved to Canada. Both were convinced those suits that night at the W Hotel were hacking their computers, wiretapping their phones, and were cause for retreat and retirement to the bipolar low country.

Jude is the founder and principal of a group called Womenstanding (one word). Jude explains on her website, Womenstanding.com, "In August 2006, with the ongoing intensity of the wars and the profound loss of human life, each Sunday afternoon my granddaughter, Gabrielle [then eight, now eighteen years old] stand in quiet contemplation at freeway on-ramps, exits, bridge overpasses carrying white flowers [roses carnations and lilies] as a statement and demonstration for peace."

By the time Gabrielle aged out of this grandma-possessed period in her young life and learned manipulation by proxy, Jude added a used pair of black combat boots, laced together, to accompany on the standing contemplations, everywhere she went like vacation, out to dinner, on the bus, to the bathroom, through airport security, and to the moon for all I know. For a period, she retreated on the cause. Maybe it's been the political environment, or perhaps it's her million, but most recently, those boots were back in commission with baby shoes for the inauguration of Donald Trump in 2016. She was at the

Women's March the day after to protest and promote many related, yet to be determined, causes, injustices, and rights.

Privately owned prisons, correctional centers being filled with illegal immigrant children with their owners paid $750 per child per day by the US government, is her new cause in 2019. It really is all our cause. It is an answer to the rest of us who feel impotent to cause change beyond the voting booth.

Today the *Womenstanding* website states, "We have assembled a small group of individuals who stand on corners, freeway overpasses, exits, in front of Federal buildings, gates to military bases dedicated to presenting a message of peace."

Lately, the familial conversations Jude and I have been on the phone from Fremont to her house in SE Tacoma. We talked a few days before the Women's March. She asked if she could spend the night.

Gabrielle voted for Donald Trump. I had a falling-out with my second cousin Gabrielle and her mother, Anna, my first cousin, over the Trump candidacy in an argument on Facebook and with subsequent need for "unfriending."

The argument started with Hillary Clinton, then candidate for president, and Benghazi, then to dialogue about the possible first husband, a "rapist," residing in the White House.

Disappointed, I argued Trump's supporters were the unemployed, underemployed, uneducated, and women threatened by the breaking of the last glass ceiling. I amplified their daughter's chance to have a female role model. I even played the grandma card. "What would our grandma Edith say?"

I found myself at this intersection or convergence of light and dark, politics, the generations, hope and disgust, and ambivalence and action and yes, temporary impotence and right here in the center of the universe.

I watched about five minutes of the Trump inauguration on local television. My fingers covered my eyes like feeling the need to turn away from a train wreck. If we don't become more vigilant, we are witnessing the end of an empire.

On the Saturday morning of the Women's March that eventually included a million local citizens, Jude called. She would be joined by granddaughter Gabrielle, then eighteen, and Gabrielle's new, twenty-year-old boyfriend (and oh yes, the boots and now the baby shoes). They would take the bus from Tacoma to Seattle. We had no concept of the undisclosed demonstration route through downtown Seattle nor a time we could meet up. Jude, in true-to-character fashion, suggested a See's Candy Store at Westlake Center. Big picture plan and neither of us thought to drill down on the specifics.

That night late, I sent the following e-mail:

Dear Aunt Jude:

I thought about driving my car home from Allan's this morning, picking up my bike, and riding it downtown. I woke up in an ambivalent daze—the kind I get more frequently, where I say yes to anything, without thinking it through to execution. My legs felt like I was standing on a couple of peg stumps. Without thinking through how to join the Women's March, meet you at a See's Candy Store at Westlake Center at a to be determined time and not get caught in the crush, and knowing I had to clean up my place for your visit. And since you not having an ability for phone contact and landline ways, well, I fucked up.

In my head, I figured you would just come to my place in Fremont. Then, all the doubts and empathic projections entered my head and amplified the angst. Did I leave you stranded? I didn't divulge my location. I should stay put here because if I left, you'd arrive at an empty home, etc. etc. I am sorry, I am sorry. It is better that I stood on the sidelines with my old man, school teacher impatience for crowds, traffic, and politics, than subject the unwitting to my voice. By all accounts, the spirit of the event was life and democracy affirming.

I did take the time to ready things for an enjoyable visit. Last night, when you wrote that Gabrielle and her boyfriend were accompanying you, I welcomed the thought and compliment you for encouraging her participation. I remembered you spoke on the phone the other night that Gladys' Mitsubishi Galant might be an excellent utility for her. On the outside chance and opportunity, I took the car to the late-night car wash and detailed it out for you and them to consider. And if a "Fit" to mutual needs met, you'd be driving it home. I need to communicate my thoughts more than over-think them to myself.

You could eat dinner off my floors, and my place sparkles now.

It's 9:30 PM now, I am sorry

But back to that Historical day for Seattle, the United States, and World and Women Standing...

Proud to be related.

Love,
Bill

Quite possibly, my finest display of passive-aggressiveness by me in print?

The next day, I received this e-mail from Jude:

OMG, Bill, never ever be concerned if we somehow seem to miss something that was previously scheduled, I'd hope in all these years we, of all people, have a clear understanding of who the other truly is...

141

The kids were late getting here, which shifted out meeting time by over an hour and a half, and I thought I'd shared verbally with you, "not to worry about anything on this day" as it will be as it will be. Knowing you had some deep concerns with the path not being perfect for us, makes me a little sad, honey! Our ongoing dialogue and kindness w/one another is all that is important, Bill, really it is.

So, with that stated, what an extraordinary uplifting day where 110,000 of us gathered just in our Seattle alone, WOW. We filtered in at Pioneer Square in a flow that had its own inertia in place (around 12:50 p.m.) I realized the possibility of you and me meeting needed to be left to the universe, Bill, and hoped you would hold the same awareness in your inner being. Never worry when it comes to me, never!!!!! Life's patterns of shifting have taught me this, and I now hold close this awareness as a trusted traveling companion. *Gabrielle's phone had lost is power, so we were in some ways at the whim of this powerful women's movement.

Gabrielle has been, in many ways, intellectually traumatized by Anna's politically fascist mindset, and at times, found distress in the signs during the march, not so much as to say, "let's go home," but more of an unclear and ungrounded understanding of the facts. She even made mention at one point of pondering how the crowd would respond if she had a sign stating: "Remember Benghazi." My only response was a reminder of how in 2011, the Republicans had defunded the embassies all over the world and that it was not as simple as had been portrayed to her.

We did go to Fremont, dear nephew, and since our physical connection remained as a shadow, enjoyed a meal at the neighbor's restaurant with the peanut sauce Gab loves. They so enjoyed seeing her etc. It was a fantastic day all the way around, other than us not meeting in person. Bill know this; we were connected along with the multi-millions all over this Pale Blue Dot!

So, sorry for your duress, truly I am.

Love and peace, always,
"Aunt" Jude

The three of them made it to Fremont that evening, almost "spitting" distance away from me at the neighbors' Thai restaurant. But there was no visit that night to my spotless home.

The next day, Sunday, I was in a funk. This time mad, mad at myself, hurt, and perplexed. I left the house for about an hour to visit my friends at the Fremont Sunday Market.

Later that Sunday evening the next day, after taking out the recycle, I come up the steps and see a tattered white rose attached to my front door.

I try to recall who might have left it. I faintly remember *Womenstanding* and check Jude's website. "Stand in quiet contemplation at freeway on-ramps, exits, bridge overpasses, carrying white flowers [roses, carnations, and lilies] as a statement and demonstration for peace."

A new era begins for us all. But it is me that has more to learn.

Halloween 2008, Gabrielle, Henry, and Aunt Jude.

Spirit Killers Appear: Off-Center in the Center of the Universe

Summer 2018

This is the part of my story I thought I'd never have to write. Most of the others in this Chautauqua from Fremont are spirit up-worthy or spirit-neutral. Today, it's a postbroken spirit. The Spirit Killer paid a visit during the smoke fire-filled skies of Seattle, Fremont, summer. This one, mine to own, came in the form of a renter, resident, squatter from hell. Tomorrow, I'll do it again.

Benny, rock dancer, artist, monk, and unofficial mayor of Fremont had his spirit killed with a late-night ambush switcheroo. Two bros, likely from another planet, were the perps. The little one appeared first and taunted and teased Benny to the point of blows. Little bro then strategically steps out, and the big one steps in from the shadows and levies the injuries. The event caused Benny to spend five days in the ICU at Swedish Hospital for injuries from his beating. Police sketch artists paid a visit to his bedside for help to catch them and their repeated antics.

We later met up on a sunny Francis Avenue, like we always do, exchanged pleasantries, and offered each other provocative thought on our world. Word was out on the street, among neighbors, of our plights. We were facing our own demons and the post-traumatic stress that has changed our lives forever. No arguments here. We were wounded and our spirits too.

"Sometimes," I say to Benny, "more lately, I think that it is absurd to still live here."

"The time here is edgy, artsy, subterranean, and full of excesses," Benny says. "I don't know how much longer I can do this."

"What do you mean?" I say.

"My art."

I can see the disappointment on his face along with the fatigue. His body posture is instantly mimicked by me. I give my side of the story in consideration of leaving the neighborhood. He was concerned about the sidewalk closures on the wedge of his block with demolition and construction commencing any day.

"Bill, I'm a mess after what happened. It's been two weeks out of the hospital, and I still can't get centered."

"My friend and colleague," I lament. "We've been knocked off our center, punched in the kidneys, brought to our knees by what we believed to be worthwhile." We both agree this city has changed, more people, more cars, more meanness, more entitlement, more resentment, more graffiti taggers, more homeless, more cost, more trash, and less of us." Disgustedly, I continue, "I can't believe your mural on the front of the photoengraver's storefront," (recording studio) "was trashed by the taggers."

Both of us hit by spirit killers in the same week.

There was no need to tell Benny of my tribulations. He already knew all the details. Checking account fraud was my latest scar to wear like a neon sign over my head easily traced to my star boarder.

It was my open-hearted, do-gooder, pleaser self that tried to give a young man approaching forty a leg up in getting an overdue foothold in the economy as a resident and small business, albeit never incubated.

As a peccadillo from last winter reappearing as a peccadillo of summer, Markell was personable, articulate, thoughtful, helpful, and present. His bright eyes and winning smile contrasted with his ebony, athlete persona.

Recently booted from his last residence where his business partner was arrested, he was on the cusp of greatness with his urban landscaping and design business. I mentioned my next-door neighbor,

Harold Myers, had a basement room that might be rented. After all, income for Harold, who introduced me to Markell, and win-win.

They came back to me with an offer to split the $300-month rent revenue by opening my bathroom and my kitchen to Markell. Now I'm a third in the plan, that I should at least defend as initiator.

Harold, all caught up in the detail with a subconscious desire to be an indignant victim, produced a short-term sublease contract with more riders than fleas, allowing for his penchant for being overly concrete.

Subsequently, cash was received and promptly taken back by the faux tenant, result of a bad check.

Beyond the fourteen showers taken a day, missing groceries, unfound keys, Markell busied his time developing stationery, business cards, calendars, and lists. He had no jobs. Did I say piercing eyes? Markell has political astuteness, fashionability, and could cry on cue. No words, no jobs, no tools, no transportation, few contacts, few friends, few chances.

Official state business license would arrive in my mailbox along with all the spam and referrals, making mine his official residence. He had been down this road before and could easily be two steps ahead of us.

To Markell, it wasn't the use of our homes that was the issue at all, for no payment, no contributions to life here could be easily excused. But it was after we were prompted to lock him out, and he broke windows, trashed the room, trashed the furniture, destroyed two gates and fences, defecated on our porches and urinated in the yard that we realized we had one squatter from hell living in our midst.

His check-foraging and check-forging operation was sophisticated. For the energy it took to manipulate the cash generators, this man could have easily been a successful sociopathic seller of anything legal using less of his life force.

But that little factory of fake money he had wasn't discovered until the lengthy process of evicting a squatter in a city of victims, squatter-centric rights, and regulations that take precedence to any landlord or host's need for sanity, community, and accommodating.

It's an irony, I guess, good use of time to no one, to have Harold making thirteen phone calls to 911, summoning thirteen visits by the Seattle Police Department, netting multiple cars on site with the city's finest-wearing video cameras strapped to their chests. Each call stacked up the total of all the agency's incident numbers, way exceeding my need for detached anonymity.

The city website offered a link, a solution to a squatter is to give them the total of a month's rent and direct them to disappear.

Harold would have none of that nonsense, basking in the spotlight of his victimhood and need to win over. Harold's skin in the game was the rental papers. Mine was the cash it took to make good on a formal, necessary eviction process, damaged property, missing checking account funds, new checking account expenses, prescription meds, broken furniture and wiring, cost for cleanup, and bearing the responsibility for all this and the effect imposed on my neighbors.

One morning, last day of July, I woke up again on the couch, smelling smoke, like burning papers. I traced the haze and smells downstairs. Bending down and sticking my head through the broken star-shaped window, Markell and I traded imperatives! Feeling impotent, I retreated to fetch for groceries. From the Fred Meyer store, the anger steam was building between my ears and in my gut.

Returning home, opening the front door, I set the full grocery bag on the floor en route down the stairs to kick open the door and plant myself firmly as an occupant in Markell's room. My advantage was obviously surprise, his was youth, combat training, and a desire to inflict irreversible markings on the landscape.

Trading of barbs and threats continued. I showed my disgust at finding my belongings strewn about the room. I picked up one of my bath towels off the floor, and in a defiant show of superiority, I pulled the towel quick enough to lightly brush across his arm and leg. The altercation commenced lightly but with increasing intensity. He hit me with his cupped left hand so that my ear canal was dead center, causing a penetration of air to pierce my eardrum.

Temporarily dazed and confused, I struggled, the ringing in my ear now permanent. I tipped over the bed, he threw me against the floor, hitting the fireplace heater foot with my rib cage when I tried to use my phone. He took my phone and kicked it across the room.

By this time, when it felt like watching the movie, I knew this was my cue to step up the volume. One could hear my wailing, cries, Hail Marys, and mea culpas five hundred feet away as I protected my head while sitting on the floor. The police car entourage arrived. I was consoled in my confusion. We were separated to tell our sides of the story in trauma-drama details. My story omitted the smelling of smoke, and his was enough to make me the initiator.

I was arrested, handcuffed, and escorted by two officers to the SPD cruiser along the walk of shame for the neighbors to see. I stop in my tracks while one led me and the other searched me.

I spout, "Wait! I need to lock up my place!"

The third officer was sent with the assurance the job would be completed to lock front and rear doors. "We'll take care of that," I hear. They didn't.

My head not guided into the back seat of the SPD cruiser. I struggled with the behind-the-back cuffing to the holding cell at the North Precinct. It was shortly after that I boarded and disembarked the police van butt first to report for booking downtown into the King County Municipal Jail. Booking is like a scary hotel registration, one relinquishes all belongings, they are documented, and the experience is shrouded in green cotton, testosterone-powered for twenty-five men plus more, and men and women in blue to cower from, and forgettable monochromatic hues.

Something caused the television privileges to be denied this night. My emotional state anchored to the feeling of my body incarcerated while my mind and spirit were somewhere, anywhere but in that place. My eyes were either closed or staring at the floor, darting left to right.

Besides obeying every direction, my only interchange was with an experienced young dweller who would ask me each meal, "Hey, pops, you gonna eat all that?" I refrained from using the block bathroom facility for twenty-five hours until my release back to the downtown street.

City dweller, night dweller, and longest on the planet in a cell block of twenty-five men. It felt like forever, and it felt like five minutes in three acts.

Ninety seconds with my assigned attorney resulted in my release by a judge in another room. Required to appear in court the following day, upstanding old fart released, and charges dropped. I was warned by my attorney that although released, I was forbidden from returning to my home on the possibility of meeting up with my adversary, thereby breaking a no-contact order.

Weighing out the consequences of this directive and throwing caution to the wind, I was returning to *my* home.

Sitting that evening, lights out, only the light of the television lit my living room. Half asleep, late, I heard a key open the front door. It was Markell, startled as he saw me when opening the door.

"Oh, someone's here," he sheepishly observes. He addresses me, "Here's your key," as he sets it inside the door. Then, I hear, "Bill, I'm sorry. I'm really sorry." As the door and this chapter closes, I don't expect the perpetrator, Markell, to resurface. Just a good hunch of mine.

Still in the shock of the traumatic drama that kicked my can, moved my cheese. It has questioned my direction in life, much like being hit over the head by a two-by-four and now how to act my age, not my shoe size.

Karma, always a copilot in my life journey, would find herself unemployed, on leave without pay, while I tried to find my center and climb back on my self-made pedestal, arm over the leg.

Two days later, Markell would be formally evicted by the sheriff, not without causing more property damage and more police calls. Almost two months later, a sheriff's detective knocked on my door with questions about Markell. MIA, multiple warrants, harassment, fraud, theft, assault, prostitution, and rape were now in the mix.

Just a few weeks ago, about eleven months from the incident, Markell again appeared at my doorstep. "No, you can't come inside. You've done enough damage here. Leave immediately, or I'm calling the police," I said, and he did.

In the subsequent self-examination and self-deploring, I would make a few new rules of engagement with the world at the foot of Francis Avenue.

- Lock the door when entering and exiting.
- Allow no strangers inside.
- Check the bank accounts for fraud every day online.
- Replace, recover, or remove any trace of use or damage.
- Talking about the perpetrator and wallowing in victimhood gives no relief but only provides the spirit killer(s) power.
- Whenever in jail, memorize a phone number to call. Without a phone contact list and our cell phones, we have no contacts at all.

Maybe I've outgrown my little oasis in Fremont?
And written on some wall somewhere, the advice:

> Calmness is mastery. You have to get to a point where your mood doesn't shift based on the insignificant actions of someone else. Don't allow others to control the direction of your life, and don't allow your emotions to overpower your intelligence.
>
> —"Quantum World—Awaken Your Mind," Facebook page

Bad news usually comes in threes, and the spirit killers visit our vulnerabilities when we think we're just trying to help.

I see less of Benny and his art these days and evenings. Sadness over the loss of the artist's and pleaser's spirits that redefining summer in our corners of the universe.

Memo to self: Keep your business clean and act your age. You are too old for this shit.

Fremont for Real

I've tried to give you my most honest storytelling, but I like Mark Twain's quote: "Never let the truth get in the way of a good story." What's it like to inhabit Fremont with "De Libertas Quirkas" (freedom to be peculiar) as our motto?

It is the kind of place where a complete stranger approaching you on the street gives you a fist bump for your colorful, attention-magnet of an outfit. But it's also the kind of place, more frequently, where someone approaching you singularly on the street pulls out their cell phone to avoid making eye contact or saying hello. Perfectly fitting to festoon your residence with odd paint combinations and trims. Artists can be temperamental but pity the poor Fremonster who takes themselves too seriously.

To the rest of the world outside the center of the universe, Fremont has an affinity for clubbing and drinking college students from the University of Washington and Seattle Pacific University. Liquor flows, and those polite kids by day turn into assholes by night. After midnight, it just gets sketchy, neighbors, homeless, revelers, and the reveled.

Sartori's marijuana store is dangerously close to my place. So dangerous, they know me by my first name, I get frequent flyer rewards and conduct informal product research for them.

These have been boom times for the Emerald City as well as Fremont. Twentysomething millennials with a lot of disposable income to pay our inflated rents and median home values approaching the stratosphere. Owning a car is increasingly more troublesome to get around and park it within reasonable walking distance of your front door with bags of organic groceries in arms. Bicycling around Fremont and the environs is made more accessible by the Burke-Gilman Trail, which circles the area and Lake Washington. It was formed by a more level-defunct railroad track, remnants of the last century. Metro has plenty of bus lines that come through here despite no plans for the light rail to come.

Nothing new, why when the low-land 1911 Fremont Bridge was eclipsed in the shadows of the George Washington Memorial Bridge (also known as the Aurora Bridge) built in 1932 that put Fremont on hard times with fewer walkabouts? This little embarrassment was impetus for its reinvention to become the center of the universe, ARF (the Artists Republic of Fremont), artist-centric, self-deprecating with tongue in cheekiness. There's the annual infamous Fremont Festival with bicyclists wearing nothing but body paint in the Solstice Parade. Think New Orleans meets the Seattle Chill.

Neighborhoods in the city of Seattle have developed their own identity over the years. Most have some community-building events and festivals, usually performed by the Chamber of Commerce and/or a nonprofit. The Fremont chamber has breakfasts for "shameless self-promotion." The Fremont Arts Council is a significant leadership force here too. It is a reminder of Fremont's recent past when hippies (or indulgent baby boomers) populated the neighborhood and civic projects. Those old hippies are more and more scarce on the streets. The Buckaroo Tavern closed, it was a longtime two-fisted drinking establishment. The other serious bar, the Dubliner, has changed hands and its name.

Newcomers speak of the famous "Seattle Chill." My theory on that is that it goes back to our early Nordic Heritage, which includes a stoicism to the elements, and our Asian heritage of a politeness that avoids causing anyone to "lose face." Our boomtown culture is changing, though, now that only one of five of us living here were born here. There is the concern the city is losing a bit of its soul as we live more densely with each other. The culture is rich here, but increasingly challenging to access.

This latest Seattle boom of 2016 to 2018 has commandeered 60 percent of the planet's construction cranes, dumped 1,700 new residents a week here, snarled or better yet, gridlocked the city streets, filled bars and restaurants, and snarled the airport. But it is still a liberal bastion in an otherwise blue state. In this boom of the tech sector, men outnumber women with a sixty-forty ratio. Just like the early days...of *Seven Brides for Seven Brothers* and Asa Mercer's ship of East Coast, single women given passage before the completion of the Panama Canal, from East Coast to West Coast. Asa Mercer was the first University of Washington president. He got that designation because back in the day, he was the only person with a college degree.

Tourists to Seattle, after getting off the cruise ships at Pier 66 and Pier 91, over a million of them each Alaska season (May through September) have three things they want to see. First, the Space Needle, second, the fish market at Pike Place that throws their stock and third, the Fremont *Troll* hiding under the George Washington Memorial Bridge, ready to devour a Volkswagen Beetle.

When I first moved here, I found myself walking down a flight of stairs at the Vintage Antique Mall. I was struck with an overwhelming feeling of déjà vu that I'd been here before. Ironically, after leaving the store, I strolled through our Fremont Sunday Market and happened upon a road sign, in green, saying, "Welcome to Fremont—Watch out for déjà vu." Other signs say, "Welcome to Fremont—Set your watch back five minutes," and "Welcome to Fremont. Somewhere between the twenty-first and twenty-third centuries."

I have called Tacoma, Ellensburg, Chelan, Bellingham, Longview, Burien, Newcastle home in my sixty-seven years. All cities in Washington State they are, but I count Fremont as my favorite. Fremont nurtures the spirit like no other. I hope to stay long after I'm gone.

Stumbling Cautiously through the Artist's Republic of Fremont

On this beautiful afternoon, it feels like fall, but it's still summer technically. I had a degree of cabin fever. Anything, any distraction at all pitched or caught to keep me from sitting down to type or pen my Fremont tales.

Denial has a hold on me along with procrastination and finally self-sabotage, a project almost complete.

Besides, it is baby Faye's birthday on Sunday. I need to look for a gift that is meaningful for a two-year-old granddaughter.

Put on the last of my clean apparel, as I'm way overdue to do laundry. Schlepped to the Laundromat and headed on foot toward the Fremont Vintage Mall as a starter but then was reminded of Portage Bay Goods and their unique gift items.

Crossing Dayton Avenue at Thirty-Sixth, the crosswalk is lit to "walk."

Intersection 36 and Dayton Avenue north. Location that I
was struck by a hit and run driver in the crosswalk.

A fellow in his early thirties is evidently going to be making a
right turn as he intensely stares at the oncoming traffic to his left,
never to the right where I negotiate the crossing of the walk. His
Honda Station Wagon is partially in the crosswalk. And it is more
efficient for me to walk in front of his car.

Eyes on the car and its driver. My little voice says, "He could
hit me. He'll look. He's going to hit me. He'll see me and stop." The
driver doesn't, and I put my arms out as he accelerates.

I am hit on the front driver's side and fly over the fender to the
street, landing on my right elbow and hip. The driver hesitates as if
to look in his rearview mirror. Lying there, I try to spot his license
number, but he speeds off. I yell out, "License number!" All I saw was
it started with the letter "B," a Washington State plate.

Several witnesses ran to my rescue; no one caught his license
plate number. They were insistent I call the medics. I feigned off that

155

idea, assured them I was okay. I'm humbled by their attentiveness. I assure again and show them I can walk.

Continuing the goal of my mission, I amble toward the center to look for a birthday gift. Along the way, I am struck by the intensity of the experience of being struck by a car and a hit-and-run driver no less. I bump into a good friend, Allan, on the way. He is an emergency medical technician. He urges me to call the police. I do.

I walk one block and sit in the sunshine at the benches placed in front of the Space Building. It's here I'll wait for the police to come as directed by the 911 operator. I sit and stare and think. I'm thankful. It wasn't me who was the driver, and he was one of the victims of the collision.

The Space Building.

"Where did the accident occur?" the operator queries.

"Thirty-Sixth and Dayton" is my response.

"Where are you now?" she asks.

"Thirty-Sixth and Evanston, one block away." I wait for the police to arrive, seemed like an eternity. I debated whether to go on about my business and stepped inside the FedEx store because I remembered they had a beverage cooler. It's where I get all my copies made once or twice a week as I give individual copies to each listener/reader in my writing class or writers group. The counter technician offers the invitation to sit inside the store if I might be more comfortable.

I hope that the driver's conscience is injured as much as my well-being, my internals, and externals. I'll tell you how it went tomorrow. "Pedestrian hit by a hit-and-run driver in city crosswalk" like a neon sign above my head. It is one more thing to chalk off on my bucket list.

I have come to believe, and I have evidence that I'm a train wreck person. I don't go looking for train wrecks or chase after firetrucks, but I seem to be standing at the corner when one occurs. And I get to deal with the subsequent effects.

The police officer arrives about forty-five minutes after the call. He asks what they can do. I again refuse medical treatment, I give him the specifics, and we depart with mutual respect. I've had enough contact with Seattle's finest in the last several years.

My faith in the kindness of people is reinforced, my disappointment in humanity is reinforced, and my trust in my own judgment is questioned, cautioned, and in need of reevaluation.

After all this, I thought, after seeing a moving YouTube sequence someone posted on Facebook today featuring J. P. Patches' granddaughter, that it had been a while since I paid homage to the statue here with costar Gertrude titled *Late for the Interurban*. It's right down on J. P. Patches Place (a.k.a. Thirty-Fourth Avenue). When it was unveiled several years ago, J. P. was still alive. I made sure to have an engraved paver stone at the foot of the statue for my grandson and me.

Truth be told, I saw J. P.'s very first KIRO-TV children's show at age seven and was a fan of the longest-running local children's show in the country. I tell people he helped raise me while my parents were asleep or working at the tavern. He was a constant, five days a week, before school and after school. I shed more tears when he passed than when my dad passed.

J. P. Patches collage, statue with Gertrude Late for
the Interurban, paver stone, ICU2TV.

JP's statue is just down the street from another famous sculpture of the dour, glum folks standing and *Waiting for the Interurban*. People like to dress them up for special occasions.

Richard Beyer's *Waiting for the Interurban.*

Patches Pals Checklist.

After J. P., I decide to keep walking so as to move my sore joints. Besides, I need a little inspiration. Down the trail to the locks, why not? Sri Chinmoy, the guru of enlightenment, has a tribute statue along the Burke-Gilman Trail down on the ship canal that connects

Puget Sound, Ballard, Fremont, Lake Union, and Lake Washington. The Ballard (Hiram Chittenden) Locks are primarily used for ships and boats traveling to and from Lake Washington and Lake Union past the fishing fleet back to Puget Sound.

The Ballard Locks is a great tourist magnet, the same era built as the Panama Canal, 1916–1917. Having seen both, I would say one can observe a lot more of the workings of locks at the Ballard location built by the Army Corps of Engineers than from a ship traversing the Panama Canal. Ballard also has a fish ladder for salmon to navigate swimming upstream to spawn. That's so long as we still have salmon. The Ballard facility was the first to connect salt water with fresh water. Buildings at the locks site are beautiful in the rare style of art nouveau.

On the way back home, I pass under the Fremont Bridge, the bridge with the most drawbridge openings of any in the country. It's painted a blue and a pink or salmon color and the neon sign on the lift tower bridge features Rapunzel letting down her hair.

The Fremont Bridge and Rapunzel neon.

I walk up the hill past Google and Adobe to the PCC grocery store. It's there at the street level of the Epicenter Building with lots of beautiful metal arts attached to the building. A full shopping cart can fetch $500.

Fremont's Epicenter Building.

I also pass the *Fremont Rocket* with our neighborhood's motto, "De Libertas Quirkas."

Fremont Rocket.

The Saturn Building is on the other side of the street. The planet is atop the four-story, mixed-use building with a Home Town Bank and three restaurants on the street floor and artists' work lofts above. Saturn's rings are solar panels delivering energy back to the grid.

The Saturn Building.

I cross the main street between the Lenin statue and the sign-post "Center of the Universe." Lenin, while controversial, attracts a lot of camera shots from the visitors here. He's got red hands one day and red fingers the next. I view it as a tongue in cheek placement here in Fremont. Some folks still get riled up over it.

The Lenin Statue.

The signpost for the center of the universe is at the actual center as we know it. Recently, some idiot tried to steal the sign and put it in her car. Photos caught her.

Actual signposts for the center of the universe
and distances to…everywhere.

Recalling my original, pre-crash mission, I stop by Portage Bay Goods, a unique collection of gift items and greeting cards. Without hesitation, I find a book suitable for granddaughter Faye titled *Here We Are: Notes for living on Planet Earth* by Oliver Jeffers. It puts the planet in perspective in the universe along with living skills. A second book offers all kinds of possibilities for this young generation titled *Galaxy Girls: 50 Amazing Stories of Women in Space* by Libby Jackson.

Portage Bay Goods in Fremont.

I want to impress upon my young granddaughter the possibilities of space travel and what is going to possibly become of this bathtub we've soiled called planet Earth. Children born now will be some of the first colonizers of outer space destinations. They should send baby boomers, my generation, one-way tickets to do the colonizing so we can go and pollute and ravage the natural resources of another planet while the young people clean up this Earth.

I walk back home to the foot of Francis, past the two murals, beautifully done with spray paint. I pass the graffiti tags everywhere on everything.

Bird at the center of the universe by *Charms*.

Monument to *Digital Divinity Mural* by Jacobson.

It's time to do laundry—it was time to do laundry about a month ago, maybe two months ago. This is just a test of your attention span.

In the next two months, my car was stolen. I was able to retrieve it using the car insurance app on my phone. Seattle police were busy, I guess, and the homing device, LoJack, was rendered useless.

A few weeks later, while parked on the street, my car was also totaled and a total loss by another hit-and-run driver, who left parts of his car body at the scene.

Bad news, disappointments, and life's tribulations, they say, come in threes. They certainly did!

Wally and the Crotch: A Ship in a Stormy Sea

Wally grew up a product of the north end of Tacoma with Episcopalian WASP values. He was born in the somehow enveloped excesses of the 1950s baby boom. But on the other hand, the excesses of the era enveloped him as well.

We met in fall 1969. Wally lived down the hall from me in Quigley Hall at Central Washington State College in Ellensburg. He was going to be taking a double major in history and political science with a minor in night time burger and pizza deliveries.

He was tall, I'd say about six feet three, he was solidly heavy-weight, loud, coke bottle glasses, scoutmaster demeanor, name-dropper, a mascot of sorts to the social groups that formed in dorm life. He suffered misogyny with women, was quick to judge, a Dan Evans Republican (fiscally conservative yet socially responsible). Wally's dad had died of a heart attack during his high school senior year. Wally was the oldest of four brothers.

His eating habits were legendary, lip-smacking, finger-licking, with audible burping and farting in the chorus of boys behaving badly, on campus and among his many friends.

We really got to know each other that summer of 1972. We had survived the lottery Vietnam War draft. I got a nepotism summer job at the paper mill as a pulp and paper relief tester. Wally got his summer job with the Seattle Parks Department, likely through the connections his dad had forged with Tacoma Public Utilities. Bottom line, we both turned twenty-one that spring and made it our goal to visit every bar, strip club, and nightclub in the region. He lived with his aunt in Fremont. I lived at home with mom, stepfather, and two younger brothers. My dad was absent and was eventually discovered after he faked his demise. He resided with his second wife, Lydia, down in North Cove on the Pacific shore as owners of the Minit Mart. We were like two firstborn looking for guidance in our world absent of fathers.

Like the two of us were searching to reinvent ourselves, Fremont was doing the same with the creation of the ARF (Artists Republic of Fremont) and building the *Troll* that devours the VW. To the degree I was introverted, Wally was equally extroverted. I needed to develop more confidence in myself, and Wally needed to become more introspective. While I stayed close to my small group of friends, Wally floated among all the groups, dabbling in each but remaining an outsider standing in the margins, without the ability to attach, maybe because of his Baby Huey, Boy Scout demeanor. Wally was loud, not booming but comfortable at foghorn decibels.

That summer before our junior year was the transition we faced after living in the dorm. We were now permitted to live off campus. He had expectations he would find a house to share with friends, but no offers to include him in the group living seemed to come his way despite his efforts. That summer, it was I who had to break it to him, this reality. We were sitting in a booth in a college tavern, where, for unknown reasons, a touchy bar staff sprayed tartar sauce at me in my cherished suede jacket. We drove over to Ellensburg, so Wally could find a solo apartment. He was always grateful that I was someone who was honest with him.

We all had college nicknames. He was Wally, I was Crotch, there was Muck, Hanky, Poindexter, and Zit. Wally kept his crew cut hairstyle despite the long hair hippies in the era. He wore Levi's when the rest of us wore bell-bottoms. He had his signature athletic shoes and short-sleeved plaid shirts. He kept reasonable hygiene despite all the complexion problems we all suffered. A friendship of convenience, location, and adequate mutual respect formed between us.

I graduated on time after four years. He took an additional year to be qualified to teach secondary social studies. While I struggled to teach high school at age twenty-two, Wally wasn't ready to settle down.

Subsequently, he never quite reached his full-career stride in those early years in the work world. His interests occupied his time as a coconspirator, best friend, and significant other to food, fast food, tater tots in armful sized bowls with ketchup and dips in lip-smacking, finger-licking depth containers. Wally became a fry cook in a chain of family dining restaurants that ascended him to manager until he punched out a customer and his future one night.

Of course, he was bound to gain weight in this environment. His weight was in the mid-two-hundred-pound range by late 2020s. Rotund clothing styles emerged for him. His love life remained ethereal and disconnected to his reality. His interests were varied—there was food, football, blackjack, strippers and poker, and food too. Wally's little green Ford Pinto had fast-food bags, wrappers, and cups as fellow passengers.

His life became one of fits, starts, and disappointments, but he lived for and remained the connecting force of all those groups he'd gone to college with. He lived vicariously through all of us.

After the restaurant biz folded, he became a professional eater and did some substitute teaching. He moved to Yakima to help his aunt and uncle.

In our forties, I lost track of Wally. I made several attempts to reach him and finally called his mother. She informed me he had fallen while a high school wrestling official and had been airlifted to Seattle's Harborview Hospital with leg and hip injuries. This gave him a leg in a brace, more seat time, and more pounds. He was broke and had to recuperate in a nursing home, embarrassed by Medicaid's ways. His mom advised me to tread lightly with him as he might not engage with me. She said to my astonishment before hanging up. "Kids are like pancakes, you know, you throw the first one away."

I called him. He agreed to see me while I was traveling throughout the state for my job. At forty-six, he seemed much more restrained in mood. He appeared, again, up on all the college gossip but detached from close friendships. While his weight was now four hundred pounds, I was struggling with my career and identity.

His mother subsequently passed away. Wally and I became closer friends and allies as we aged. He drove across the state once to be my cheerleader when I received some professional recognition at a teacher conference.

With his fry cook background, he was a real piece of work eater. When we would order dinners off the menu, he gave obsessive-compulsive instructions to waitstaff, specifying what, how, when, and all about his pending gut-filling eating expectation.

Surprise! Mom died and left him $170,000. It allowed him to buy a house in Yakima with $100,000 for the home and $70,000 for hookers. The money came down from his grandfather, who had been the founder of an Alaskan bank.

On one of my trips through Central Washington, I met up with him. We hit the streets of Yakima's downtown for margaritas, beers, and Mexican food. And big ol' Wally, with the hubris of hummus, told proud tales of his hooker conquests. Lisa and Julie were his lovers to his star customer status. He was crushed and lonely when the money ran out along with their collective affection.

He didn't know how much he weighed at this point because the traditional bathroom scale was outgrown, and after the doctor's office scale, his only other weight measure was the truck scales. He estimated it to be between 450 and 475. Driving was becoming an issue for him, having long enough arms and legs to accommodate his rotund form in the driver's seat of his big sedan. After dinner, we returned to his home, inebriated I was, and I noticed his furnishings. In a smart-ass tone, I noted a reproduction on his wall of a sailing ship navigating stormy seas. I blurted out, "Wally, that's a cool picture. You need to leave it to me in your will."

I was struggling with my sexual identity, and my marriage and career were in the bucket. We took guy weekend trips to casinos and Las Vegas. I "came out" to Wally on one trip to Lincoln City, Oregon. He was the second person I trusted with this revelation after my brother. He was in disbelief and disturbed by the news, but he said what I needed to hear.

He said to me in a tone that is timeless in my memory today, "I may not agree with you, but you will always be my friend." Once said, "Let's go eat" or "Squeet" followed the declaration. We did, steak and shrimp casino buffet. The subject of my sexual identity never came up again, except when he compensated his sensitivity.

By the time we were well into our fifties, our politics had grown very polarized, thanks, in part, to talk radio. We would agree to disagree, but usually, that was after a shouting match, and one of us hanging up the phone on the other. The irony, this staunch Republican was now on disability. His weight was now over five hundred pounds. His health was page 1 of his life story.

Mobility grew harder for Wally. We would talk on the phone less frequently. In 2004, he called me around Christmastime. The state of Washington would be paying for him to have gastric bypass surgery. After spending his last dollars on a hooker who called him "Buddha," he invited me to breakfast at his hotel. Right before, he called me that morning to ask if it was okay that we eat room service. He had no clothes that fit him anymore. He greeted me at the door in his underwear. Our "last" meal together was not balanced, sitting across the table from my friend, who now weighed in at 540 pounds. Our meeting took on sentimental tones, and I tried to reassure him that life would be much better. The next day, he had the surgery.

In recovery and in the following year, he dropped over two hundred pounds from his frame. He became a full-time substitute teacher in the Selah School District. His annual Christmas newsletters took on a different tone. I could see his satisfaction with his life and career. The grace and his redemption in his written words convinced me he'd finally hit his stride.

In late spring of 2006, I received a call from his younger brother, Mike, informing me of Wally's death. His struggle with food, likely fueled by his thirst for life, kept him stuffing his protracted grapefruit-sized stomach. His stomach lacerated, causing local doctors to induce a nine-day coma, his insides open during the process. He surprised doctors with his progress. They brought him to consciousness, and it was then necessary to get him up, walking as part of his recovery. A blood clot dislodged, and he subsequently died.

A funeral service was held in Selah at his church. I knew I had to attend the service. I also felt the necessity to grow up and to get up and speak at his memorial. Arriving in the parking lot that day, I was just getting out of my car when I was met by his brother Mike. After my condolences and pleasantries, Mike said in passing to me, "Bill, be sure to see me before you leave today. Wally had something he wanted you to have." I struggled to hold back the tears.

The church was full of family, friends, colleagues, parents, and students. We honored Wally's life and memories of the connections he made for all of us throughout our years. My little speech elicited "Amen" several times from participants.

After the service, I didn't get much chance to pay my respects to his family but found myself engaging with another college friend, old roommate, and basketball player. His weight had also ballooned up postcollege. As we parted, I told him how happy I was to see him but that I didn't want to attend his funeral also.

Ship in Rough Seas art.

I met Wally's brother, Mike, outside the foyer of the church. It was there he gave me the painting of the ship in stormy seas. Tears flowed all the way back, driving home over the Cascade mountains. I hang the picture proudly in my living room and think of Wally often. I would give anything to be able to ask him today who he thinks should play him in the movie.

Wally.

Foot of Francis Land God's Story as Told by a Shirttail Relative

Most renters have a love, hate, and fear relationship with their landlord. I have admiration and respect when describing Brian Smithson, the land god of our Francis Avenue fourplex. Living here for the past ten years, my only fear was he would raise the rent to current market value or, worse yet, surprise us one day that he sold it to a developer hell-bent on tearing it down, digging a hole, and putting up a multistory mixed-use building in its place with that cardboard-siding, particle board cookie cutter walls, and a flat roof. The flat roofs make *no* sense in this Pacific Northwest soggy climate, by the way.

Brian, the land god and his spouse, Cami, have a history here in Fremont, and I turned to them as this collection of tales of the center of the universe neared completion. The history of this corner of Fremont and their acquisition, stewardship, investment in residential and commercial property contributes to the spirit here among the denizens, customers, visitors, and dogs.

You can be tapping your toes and bobbing your head here at the foot of Francis. The music of the Nectar Lounge bands adds the drumbeat to the tempo of life. If it weren't for the goddamned litter it'd be a slice of heaven. Nighttime revelers leave a residue unsupervised. 'Tis part of the charm. Brian's son, Jed, has established his Nectar Lounge as a venue of distinction for acts on the way up and the way down the charts. Brian enjoys taking in the reggae concerts there. Me, I take in the acts from the street or feel the beat from my pillow.

Residents, denizens can judge from the evidence they see, but we love it.

A few years ago, I somehow pissed off Jed by trying to get an interview to write a story about the Nectar Lounge for the Fremocentrist.com, our neighborhood news source. As angry young man owning and operating a nightclub year after year, he scolded me as I walked in the front door and approached the bar. "If you don't quit bothering me, I'm going to get a restraining order against you." It was my fourth attempt to meet with him.

I told him in my anger, "I will *never* speak to you again."

I thought I wrote the incident off and questioned my confidence in composing stories. But my mission was to write a puff piece on him and his club. Not exactly hard-hitting journalism here. It was a short-termed no-speak period. We are a collective that looks out for neighborhood. Jed is quite the businessman and, I assume, a pillar of the music scene to attract the quality of performers he does on his stage at Nectar Lounge.

I've been thrown out of the dog bar, Norm's, and the soccer-crazed bar, George and the Dragon as well, both times related to take-out food transactions. The insight here drops right down on me. Aging know-it-alls like me served by day-to-day operators toughened by the antics of the alcohol-consuming student, tourist, music-, dog- and soccer-loving communities makes for high burnout factors in doing business. Their message: "Just shut up and order drinks. I won't make your life harder if you don't make mine and especially if you don't fit our customer demographic."

Life in the teenage years of the twenty-first century, here at the foot of Francis, springs up Francis' leg where time wounds all heels at the intersection of bottle in front of me and frontal lobotomy. It's time we put some perspective on Francis' teen years, 2000–2020.

Taking a step back from the day to day and looking under the skirts at the foot of Francis to consider the evolution, sustainability, viability of Fremont falls in the laps of the entrepreneurs, the stewards, the visionaries, the risk-takers and the rewards takers, the empire building, the absentee landlords, the trust-babies, the rogues, the reformers, the corporate, the noncorporate, and the nonsuits.

It takes a special breed of individual, like Brian and his family, to be in the game for the long term and fight off the developers, not parcel up to sell and make a fast dollar, in this, Seattle's boomtown era of the of the early twenty-first century. I admire the stability, especially using my live-for-today, immediate gratification lifestyle lenses.

This native of the Evergreen State, the banker's son, just out of college with his east coast acquired MBA degree, Brian rolled into town during Seattle's bust cycle characterized by the billboard here in the 1970s that read "Will the last person leaving Seattle—Turn out the lights."

Brian went to work for his ex-father-in-law in Fremont's Baby Diaper Service, a laundry service for soft to the tush cloth diapers.

His ex-father-in-law gave him a leg up with a ten-year contract to purchase the business. Fremont was a neighborhood in the 1970s that was a "hippie hollow"—light industrial, single-family homes, low rents, and a place overlooked in the shadows of the George Washington Memorial Bridge / Aurora Bridge / Highway 99 Bridge.

Customers today would be surprised to know that the Ballroom was the home of the laundry that cleaned the cloth that softened the rears, at its peak, of over fifteen thousand babies. With three massive industrial washing machines, a legion of employees and a fleet of delivery trucks. The Ballroom's covered outdoor seating area was a drive-through portico for customers to drop off dirty and pick up clean.

In the large house at the foot of Phinney, now home to Kaosamai Thai Restaurant, were the offices and employees manning the phones, producing a monthly magazine for their new mothers giving advice, techniques, and reassurance to those adjusting to their new lives and roles as parents.

Subsequent success was also attained by building a second Baby Diaper Service laundry facility in Tacoma 35 miles south of Seattle, right next door to the Almond Roca-Mountain Bar maker, Brown & Haley. My dad, Bill Crossman Sr., told the story that while at the controls of train engines for the Milwaukee Road, my grandfather, William McKinley Crossman, would stop the train on the tracks directly below where the women making daily the Brown & Haley, would shower them with Mountain Bars.

At the nexus of Fremont's reinvention of itself and subsequent corporate takeover of the baby waste collection industry, Brian and Cami saw the future. Their labor of love and service to family was eclipsed by the convenience of the plastic-intensive, earth-unfriendly, landfill-destined, use-once-and-toss, rash-promoting disposable diaper.

It's a lot like video killing the radio star, Amazon-killing retail, and our cell phone killing our camera, wristwatch, and brain. Enter the new era. Enter the twenty-first century and enter the postinternet era.

Around the corner on Francis for the do-it-yourself crowd was the Speed Queen Coin Laundromat. Residents in my building, the funky fourplex, complained of the rumble of the washing machines, and the Smithsons purchased it, maybe to appease them or shut them up. The fourplex today plus an older home up the block are the last two remaining original residential structures on this block from Thirty-Sixth Avenue to Thirty-Ninth Avenue. Actually, this fourplex was moved from the path of Interstate 5 in the 1960s. Plopped down on concrete blocks, the basement left unfinished for many years.

Suzie Burke, Fremont's Queen of the Land Gods, takes credit for connecting the Smithsons to the Merrill Family Trust, owners of the Safeway Building. The Smithson's Baby Diaper Service was "busting at the seams" when the laundry was at its zenith. Burke's Empire, rumor has it, was the rest of commercial Fremont. Well, maybe not all of it but a nice chunk of Fremont. Queen Suzie was overseer of the family empire that started lumber mills, commercial and industrial property with earthmovers and earthshakers a century ago.

Having talked with Suzie, next in the Smithsons's future was acquisition of the building at the corner of Thirty-Sixth Avenue and Dayton that was originally built to be a Safeway Grocery Store and later became a cashier checker training center for Safeway's chain of stores. Today, it is home to well-established and popular Roxy's Diner, the Back Door (a bar for adults), and Norm's (yes, a bar for dogs). In the interim years, this building was also home to Rain City Video, a cigar store, and a fish store.

Brian pays tribute to wife's, Cami's, "sixth sense" for selection of tenants for long-term success and stability. Once the laundry business ended, she also oversaw the design and remodel of the space, transforming it to the beautiful Ballroom. Customers line up down the block to gain entry on weekend nights to revel, play pool, and be seen.

I'm fortunate I passed Cami's muster when I inquired about renting an apartment from them. I'll never forget her words, "You know what you're getting into, living here?"

"Yes," I responded earnestly.

"Then *don't* call us!" which I took as a message to be self-sufficient and only call for the big stuff, like the sewer backing up into the basement twice in eleven months. Although this vibrant neighborhood of revelers and the reveled may be bothersome to some, living here is a gift in my opinion.

Brian has said he's keeping the family's real estate holdings intact and that his children will decide the fate after he and Cami are gone—uncommonly decent, uncommonly Christian, uncommon philosophy by today's standards.

My aunt Jude lived here many years before me. Before that, her daughter Anna lived here as well with her daughter, Gabrielle. Gabrielle is remembered fondly by all the neighbors as a young girl with more than her share of curiosity. My cousin Anna married Jason, Brian and Cami's son. And that is our shirttail relative connection. All three generations of us that started this story when I bumped into Aunt Jude and Gabrielle at the counter of the store across the street.

Sometimes in Fremont there are, and this is one, center of the universe magical moments dished up to improve our lives. Fremont, the Smithsons, and the family connections here have enriched my years beyond full measure.

Defending My Life

In all the commotion of my earthbound demise and the heavenly transition to the afterlife, I realize it is just like Paul Simon's song "The Afterlife." I do hear harps and angels as I bask in the warm white light above me with celestial shades and tints.

From the song's lyrics,

> After I died and the makeup had dried,
> I went back to my place.
> No moon that night, but a heavenly light
> Shone on my face.
> Still, I thought it was odd there was no sign of
> God
> Just to usher me in.
> Then a voice from above, sugar-coated with love,
> Said: Let us begin.
> You got to fill out a form first
> And then you wait in the line,
> You got to fill out a form first
> And then you wait in the line.

—Paul Simon's "The Afterlife"

"But, *but!*" I say. I do protest too much, I hate those lines, but this is one time I figure, I really must be patient and just wait.

"*Quiet!*" the voice says. "You'll get your chance to lay out your case."

180

As the line snakes around this holding area, clearly a mess from all the construction and expansion, my favorite angel, who visited me in my dreams, appears. I now see all those times I was visited to give me guidance, some of which I listened to, some of which I rejected, and some of which I never heard. My angel will serve as my pro bono counsel in Saint Peter's Court of Review at the Heavenly Marriott Hotel just outside those Pearly Gates.

"Well, I'll be," I mutter under my breath. "Marriott, eh?" The Mormons *do* have a stake here. The questions were on the tablet, not a stone tablet but more like my Amazon Kindle. *But* I just had to think, and the answers appeared on the screen. We proceed though the big four questions:

1. What are your regrets in this past life?
2. What are your contributions to humanity?
3. What will be your legacy? and
4. State your priorities on a numbered scale of one to five for your next assignment.

And this was followed by a disclaimer, "All decisions made by this court are arbitrary and can be overturned at any time. Christian, Muslim Buddhist, atheist, or Jewish, get over those earthly tribal tangles."

The reality hits. "*This is it!*" I say to myself. "*And my next assignment? What's up with that?*" Now I'm here at my defining rite of passage.

My longtime quest for authenticity demands I tell the truth—no sales, no sales techniques, no exaggerations. The angel advised me to be economical in my choice of words, direct, humble, without trying any smart-ass humor as I look up from the base of these clouds toward the skies in this processing center for the universal court of first and last detainees.

I then hear my processing begin. "For the record, list your regrets in this past of life of eighty-five years on earth."

"Your Honor, Eminence, uh..." My voice cracks nervously, I proceed. "I didn't care enough for the planet, the Earth, Mother."

I'm feeling a good start and see nonverbal approvals. "I wish I had selected better parents." I begin to play the victim's card.

"*Oh, boo-hoo.*" I hear a chorus of voices say. One heckler chides me, "This is your judgment day. It's not the *Oprah Show.*" Now I'm really on pins and needles. At least they couldn't see me sweat, I think.

"I wish I had taken more time with my four children."

"*Cha-ching!*" I hear, like a game show, followed by, "*Good answer!*"

"I wish I had taken better care of my stuff."

"*Good answer!*" I hear, it shows humility.

"I wish I had taken less recreational drugs."

"There's another *no-brainer*," I hear.

"I'll have a flat stomach in my next life. I'll take better care of my teeth. I regret buying those penny loafers on sale in the 1980s that were one size too small that created my bunion. And that year, I didn't wash any dishes. I need a do-over."

I then hear, "All well and good," followed by, "on the plus side of this ledger, what were your contributions to humanity?"

This part, I think, is *really* making me tense. I start to read from my notes and remember I just need to "chill" and project my confident teacher voice.

"I hopefully improved the economic lives of thousands of students in my career of thirty-three years. I helped raise my children, and all are remarkable, successful, productive humans without a serial killer among them."

"You haven't contributed much to your religion," I hear from the voice.

"Au contraire," I say. "In all due respect, my contributions were used to help others, not divide them."

"You didn't save much money."

"But," I say, "I was generous, don't you think?"

No response.

"There's your mother…?" The voice trails off, and *now* I feel defensive.

"It was her deceptions and manipulating I paid for." That's all I could say.

"Your father, you didn't honor him either, even after his last-ditch apologies to make right."

I say, "He was missing in action physically, a sociopath, a self-centered politician."

"Did you seek justice?"

I pause at that question, searching through the files in my brain, slowly rolling my eyes back.

"Yes," I say. "I believe I improved the lot of many in my charge and in the universe." I then say, "May I submit my receipts for my donations made to the Human Rights Campaign, Environment Washington, Greenpeace, J. P. Patches, and the Democratic Party?"

"*Not admissible.* There are no taxes here. Any records of theft?"

"No, but I guess karma has been a good teacher," I say.

A voice from accounting pipes in, "Oh, there was that matter of the slush fund you had from conference funds when you were in Olympia."

"But it was the bookkeeper that got caught," I say. Now I sound defensive. "I had receipts for everything. It was for expenses out of the circle of state code. It was to improve the lives of ten thousand high school students and their teachers."

"Fidelity, speak to us of fidelity," I hear.

"Twenty-six years, I experienced fidelity in my marriage and in my passion for my profession of thirty-three fucking years [sorry, but it's habit and rolls off the tongue so well to say that]. I tried to follow the 'Campsite Rule' to leave others in better shape than I found them."

"What's next for your soul?" I hear in a tone that indicated I was getting a positive review. I ponder, shuffle through my notes.

"Here's my summation. It's been a good life. I realized my purpose, loved those around me, and it is said one becomes immortal through teaching. I'm a volunteer for many community groups. I pick up the garbage on our street. I am always prompt. I took risks in the name of the greater good.

"If I felt there was urgency, I could get dramatic when I needed to make a point.

"I took time to reflect, took time to cry, took time to accept, took time to laugh, and took time for myself and time to serve others.

"Don't forget all those random acts of kindness, right up to the end.

"I kept it real.

"Never did I sell out.

"My heart was behind my efforts."

"Very well," the voice cuts me off. "Enjoy your sabbatical. And don't be gone too long, amen, all beings. And there's one last item. You haven't earned enough rewards points for permanent residency here. So what are your priority assignments for your next life?"

"I tell ya," I respond, "I promise to compose a list after a month's sabbatical. I'm tired." I feel compelled to earnestly respond after a pregnant pause... "This and my past lives are a trajectory toward enlightenment. I'll go wherever I'm needed and do the most for the greater good. But to your schedulers, I ask. I like the idea of colonizing another planet, or going back in time, before cell phones. A place I could help rewrite the scripts that create equality, harmony with nature without red states and blue states, and bigots, bimbos, charlatans, consultants on contract, and especially the judgmental."

"Ding!" I hear. The score appears above the pearly gates, "8.9, or an A- or B+," the gate opens without fanfare, and I hear, "*Next!*" as I proceed.

I smile in relief and think to myself, "There really is an afterlife!"

I say to those from my past lives I recognize, "Hey, let's go get a drink!"

About the Author

bill crossman, author, artist, collector, curmudgeon, Fremonster, storyteller, music
bulimic, raconteur, rake, grandfather,
ADHD-inspired, gardener, thrift store pre-
hoarder, and adult literacy tutor. He has his
master's degree in BS detector studies and a
minor in gullibility. Karma, a former associ-
ate, and spiritual guide, describes Crossman
as "lacking the willingness to hear you
because he's too busy thinking of the next
words out of his mouth."

He's writing these stories in the third act of his life and has been
that has been through all the isms—idealism, realism, pragmatism,
and cynicism. He follows the sage advice of the Lego Man to express
oneself creatively every day. He believes it is cheaper than a shrink.
Formerly a straight man and a late bloomer to being gay offer him
insights into the origins of his ambivalence.

Crossman is a native of Washington State. Born in Tacoma,
he's lived in other cities around the state, including Ellensburg,
Chelan, Bellingham, Longview, Burien, and Newcastle before finding Fremont.

By looking out those eighteen windows in his apartment in
the funky fourplex, formerly home to his aunt Jude and cousins, he
delves in a life that many would describe as a train wreck. His voice
is his own, and he's a seeker of truth, except when it gets in the way
of a great story.

CPSIA information can be obtained
at www.ICGtesting.com
Printed in the USA
JSHW050910150121
10920JS00003B/10